The Christ *They* Knew

Entering The Jesus Experience

Doug Belton

Table of Contents

Dedication

As this book is published, I want to acknowledge three men whom the Christian community lost over a 13-month period from January 2025 to February 2026. All three were giants in their respective fields and made a profound impact on my spiritual life. I dedicate this book to their memory because each of them, in their own way, demonstrated a deep intimacy with Jesus that should inspire anyone serious about their Christian journey.

Let us sing the songs of Ron Kenoly with passion in our churches and may the spoken and written words of Voddie Baucham and Paul Shepherd be quoted accurately and enthusiastically from our pens, pulpits, and lecterns. May we all aspire to live lives as full and blessed as theirs.

Paul Sheppard Nov. 29, 1957 – Jan. 25, 2025. Pastor of Destiny Christian Fellowship in Freemont California.

Voddie Baucham Mar. 11, 1969 – Sept. 25, 2025. Author, Educator, and president of Founders Seminary in Cape Coral, Florida.

Ron Kenoly Dec. 6, 1944 – Feb. 3, 2026. Christian worship leader, singer, and songwriter.

Prologue

I invite you to join me as we travel back in time to the days when our Lord and Savior conducted His earthly ministry. The purpose of this expedition is to discover the Jesus His 12 closest friends, His mother, His siblings, the religious leaders of the day, and the disciples who were not part of His inner circle knew. We will invoke the entire Bible to paint a picture which reveals how those who encountered Jesus would likely have experienced being in His presence. My hope and my prayer is that we can move beyond loving Jesus as an abstract, corporate, construct, to loving Him as a person with a unique, compelling, personality. I want our tour through the earthly ministry of Jesus to create an awareness of Him that evokes images of warmth, humor, brilliance, and awe. I want us to emerge from this experience with an ability to contemplate Jesus as someone we know personally and intimately.

If you already have a deep abiding love for Jesus, my hope is that your love will be enhanced by what you read here. If you love Jesus because He is your Lord and Savior, but you feel as though a close intimate relationship with Him is missing in your life, my hope is that through this journey you will personalize your relationship with Him. If you have never known Jesus, my prayer is that through this journey you will get to know Him and be inspired by the Holy Spirit to follow Him as so many have over the last two millennia.

The story of Jesus's ministry picks up after the Jews had returned to the land, which by the first century was under Roman occupation. In addition to being under Roman dominion, the Jews were burdened with the yoke placed upon them by the religious authorities. The Jews were ready for the deliverer whom prophesy had promised, and over the years many men had stepped up and claimed to be the Messiah. However, Jesus was different. Our journey in this book will be one of discovering what the people of the first century saw, heard, and experienced, which made Jesus different from the others. We want to know what it must have felt like to have been living under the yoke of oppression and then encounter Jesus after so many disappointments.

We will examine ten facets of Jesus that were experienced by those He spent time with while He was here on earth. The ten facets of Jesus we will focus on are:

1. Jesus as the heir of all things
2. Jesus as God
3. Jesus as the Son of God
4. Jesus as a leader
5. Jesus as a friend
6. Jesus as a teacher
7. Jesus as a preacher
8. Jesus as a pastor
9. Jesus as an activist
10. Jesus as Messiah

To get the most out of this journey I encourage you to imagine yourself living in the first century Ancient Near East under Roman rule. At this point in Jewish history the people had:

- Endured 400 years of bondage in Egypt.
- Been led out of Egypt by Moses.
- Spent 40 years in the wilderness
- Gone in and occupied the promised land
- Gone through the period of the Judges

- Gone through the period of the monarchy.
- Gone through the period of the divided kingdom
- Survived the northern kingdom of Israel being carried off by Assyria.
- Survived the southern kingdom of Judah being carried off by Babylon.
- Endured a 400-year intertestamental period where God was silent.

God's people remained under Roman dominion after years of being under the rule of Assyria, Babylon, and Persia. Now, a new face came on the scene making proclamations they had never heard, doing things that had never been done, and challenging the establishment in ways no one had ever considered. Jesus had a whimsical, magnetic, and irresistible personality which could not be ignored by those seeking hope or by those who greatly benefited from maintaining the status quo. If you can imagine yourself transported into this reality, encountering the Lord and Savior we read about on the pages of the Bible, consider how you might have been affected by Him as you experienced these ten facets of His being. This is the question we will ask ourselves throughout this journey as we draw closer to the One they knew and enter the Jesus experience. Unless otherwise noted, all scripture quotations will come from the NASB version of the Holy Bible.

Chapter One

Jesus The Heir of All things

This chapter will explore the many ways Jesus established Himself as the Heir of all things, reclaiming territory that had been usurped over the course of many years by the religious authorities of the 1st century. Jesus began His earthly ministry at a time when the Jewish people were hungry for spiritual leadership, and He often clashed with the Sanhedrin, a sort of religious governing body for the Jewish people. We will explore the ways in which Jesus used these conflicts to demonstrate through scriptures how He is the ultimate authority and arbiter of God's people as the Heir of all things.

The Jewish nation began with Abram, who became Abraham, and it was expanded through Abraham's grandson Jacob, who became Israel. Jacob went into Egypt with about 75 people, including his 12 sons, their wives, their children, and their servants. The same group of Hebrews left Egypt 400 years later about 1.5 million strong. Moses led them through the wilderness and Joshua brought them into the promised land. Moses and then Joshua were the first prophets and judges of Israel, and the time of the judges continued through Samuel.

Throughout the time of the judges and through the time of the Monarchy there have always been prophets who spoke to the people for God. The prophets often began their prophecy by saying, "*Thus says the Lord.*" After the Northern Kingdom of Israel was carried into captivity by Assyria and the Southern Kingdom of Judah was carried off by Babylon, there was a 400-year intertestamental period during which no prophecy or scripture was recorded or included in the Biblical canon.

The title of this chapter is derived from Hebrews 1:1-2, "***God, after He spoke long ago to the fathers in the prophets in many portions and in many ways, in these last days has spoken to us in His son, whom He appointed heir of all things, through whom also He made the world.***" When I asked myself who Jesus was to the people around Him, I read Hebrews 1:1-2 several times, and it jumped off the page at me. The Jews were expecting a Messiah, and they absolutely got one, but Jesus was and is more than a Messiah; He is the Heir of the living God, who not only speaks for God, but He is God. Unlike the prophets, Jesus never needs to preface His words with, "*Thus says the Lord*" because He is the Lord. Therefore, one way to see Jesus through the eyes of those who walked along with Him is to see Him as the Heir, the One who was and is to come, the One who shall inherit the Kingdom.

The through line of all sixty-six books of the Bible, from Genesis 1 through Revelation 22, is that God created the world through the agency of His Son, that man separated himself from God through sin, and that as the Heir of all things, Jesus is the redeemer of man. John 14:6 tells us that Jesus is the way, the truth, and the life, and that no one comes to the Father except through Jesus. As we read the Bible, we enter the Jesus experience by seeing what those who walked with Him saw and understanding how they began to realize they were in the presence of The Heir.

Although there are a number of theories speculating on who wrote Hebrews, we don't know for certain who wrote this book of the Bible, and we may never know. However, I want to offer us some framework for understanding these first two verses in the first chapter of Hebrews. One question we might ask is, what did the writer of Hebrews see in the pre-incarnate Jesus, the incarnate Jesus, or the risen Jesus, which caused him to describe Jesus as the "***Heir***" of all things?

Let's take a closer look at these first two verses of Hebrews. Hebrews 1:1 reads, He, [God] spoke long ago to the ***fathers*** in [Through] the ***prophets***. Hebrews 1:2 reads, in these last days [God] has spoken to ***us*** in [Through] His ***Son***." These two verses are an incredible statement of theology which tells us that prior to the advent of Jesus, God spoke not directly to us, [The people of God], He spoke to the fathers, [Leaders] through the prophets. However, in these last days, He is speaking directly to us through His Son, Jesus. This means, we no longer need a human mediator to hear from God the Father because He has given us His Son who speaks directly to us. The balance of Hebrews elucidates this primary theme of the book, which is that Jesus is the mediator through whom we approach the throne of God. By this, we can now understand that throughout Jesus's earthly ministry, one purpose of His ministry is to be used by God to eliminate the bureaucracy and red tape of the old system in order to speak directly to His people with clarity and truth.

If this is what the writer of Hebrews believed it behooves us in this study to put ourselves in the sandals of a first century Jew, who had never known of or even considered the possibility of hearing directly from God through His Son. These first-century Jews had never considered the possibility of approaching God without the interpretative machinations of the religious rulers who did everything they could to maintain distance between God and His people so that they could stand in the gap and retain a position of significance they were never intended to have.

Viewing the life and ministry of Jesus through this lens helps us better understand why the sermons, teachings, and parables of Jesus were so often aimed at breaking down the apparatus so carefully constructed by the religious leaders to glorify themselves rather than God. Viewing the life and ministry of Jesus through this lens also helps us to understand what made Him so different, enigmatic, intriguing, and compelling to those who followed Him. In effect, as the heir, Jesus was taking that which the religious leaders had misappropriated for themselves and claiming it for Himself. Jesus was walking onto the scene and declaring rightful ownership of all that had been taken from His father.

During the earthly ministry of Jesus, to communicate a point, He would:

Teach – Jesus taught by simply answering a question. In most cases, he would answer the questions of those in his inner circle, but in some cases, he answered the questions asked by the religious authorities of the time.

Preach – Jesus would deliver discourses to large groups of people. These sermons were usually persuasive in nature.

Act – Jesus performed miracles of healing or demonic exorcism. Sometimes Jesus would cause an immediate change in something that naturally could only occur over a period of time, like changing water into wine, or causing a fig branch to immediately wither.

Speak a parable – Parables were stories told using analogies and metaphors to elucidate a particular principal. In some cases, Jesus would begin a parable by saying something like, "*The Kingdom of Heaven is Like...*" In all cases, Jesus used imagery in these parables to personalize concepts in ways that allowed the listener to apply the principal to themselves or their behaviors.

At this point I want to look at how Jesus used parables to establish his own claim as the Heir of all things. First-century Jews understood inheritance well; it was an integral component of their culture for parents to pass on something to the next generation. (Proverbs 13:22) The Jews codified laws that governed the transition of material wealth from one generation to another, so when Jesus used the concept of inheritance in His parables, the implications of what He communicated were crystal clear to those who heard what he said. I want us to look at three parables in particular where Jesus established his claim as Heir of all things, one in the Gospel of Matthew, and two in the Gospel of Luke.

The Parable of The Talents – Matthew 25:14-30

The parable of the talents is an illustration Jesus used in Matthew 24 to teach His disciples to properly differentiate between the things that were occurring at that point in time, and the things that had not yet occurred. In Matthew 24:1 Jesus came out of the temple, and the disciples who were impressed with the splendor of the temple and its architecture drew Jesus's attention to the temple buildings. Jesus began by redirecting the disciple's attention and giving them a future orientation to reorder their thinking. Jesus predicted the temple would soon be destroyed; hearing this, the disciples wanted to know when it would happen.

We have a historical perspective on these events, so we know the temple was destroyed in 70ad, but the disciples did not and could not have known this. Rather than giving the disciples dates and times for future events, Jesus gave His disciples a valuable lesson in preparedness so that instead of focusing on future dates and times, they would focus on how to live in the present time. Jesus taught this lesson by giving them a mental picture of an heir preparing to claim his inheritance, but in this picture the image was of Himself as the heir, and the inheritance being the world itself.

Jesus gave several relatable word pictures that His disciples could understand and apply, including the parable of the fig tree (Matthew 24:32-41) and the parable of the virgins (Matthew 25:1-13). Jesus did this to prepare the disciples to deal with false prophets and to keep themselves busy doing the good works they were called to do. Then in Matthew 25:14-30, Jesus told an incredible parable of the talents wherein He made several important points, and He clearly described God the Father as the creator and owner of all things, delivering His creation into the hands of His heir, Jesus.

Although the parable of the talents is written between Matthew 25:14-30, Jesus continued His thoughts from verses 31-46 to explain the judgment to come where the heir will separate those who are faithful from those who are not. In all of this, Jesus described Himself as the Son of Man (The Heir) who will separate everyone into two categories: those who were obedient to the master and those who were not. The next two parables we will look at are found in the Gospel of Luke.

The parable in Luke 19:11-27 also needs to be examined within its context. In Luke 19:1, Jesus entered Jericho, where He encountered Zacchaeus, the tax collector. Jews living in the first century hated tax collectors because they were agents of the Roman government who collected money from them, but most often they were corrupt, collecting more money than was due. The Roman officials would overlook this practice and allow tax collectors to become rich from their collections. Zacheus had heard of Jesus, and He was intrigued, so much so that he climbed up a tree just to get a look at Him.

Jesus called out to Zacchaeus while he was in the tree and invited Himself to lodge at his home. Jesus's followers were not pleased with His decision, but Jesus discerned that Zacchaeus had put his faith in Jesus, and He proclaimed that Zacchaeus and his entire household had been saved as a result. At this point, Jesus told a parable, not to share His thoughts on investment strategies or the virtues of capitalism, but to explain the comment He made in verse 10 of chapter 19, where He said, "***For the Son of Man [Jesus] has come to seek and to save that which was lost.***"

Jesus told the parable of a nobleman (An Heir) who was heading for a distant land. The nobleman gave 10 slaves one mina each with the expectation that they would use the money to earn more money for him. A mina was worth a little over $1.00, but it would be a mistake to focus on the money in this parable. In this parable, Jesus was again positioning Himself in the minds of those listening to Him as the Heir of all things, but He was not drawing an equivalency between the personality traits and the values of the nobleman and those of Himself. Jesus was trying to relate to His followers in terms they could grasp, and all of them could easily relate to the idea of an heir, traveling to a distant land to receive an inheritance, and leaving a group of trusted servants in charge of increasing his wealth as opposed to simply protecting what he already had.

The parable was used to give Jesus's followers a relatable word picture that would help them understand that, like the nobleman, Jesus will soon go away, and when He does, He will trust His servants (His followers) with that which is dear to Him (Humanity). In His absence, Jesus would expect His followers to use the gifts they have been given so that more followers will be added. Jesus was using the parable to make the point that all humanity, including tax collectors like Zacchaeus, make up a valuable harvest to God the Father, and He has given all of it to Jesus, who in turn will entrust it to us, His followers.

The last of the three parables we will look at is found in Luke 20:9-18. I again caution you not to look at these or any other parables of Jesus in isolation. Like the previous two we looked at, Luke 20:9-18 is used by Jesus to make a point about something that was going on when He told the parable. In Luke 19:45, Jesus had entered the temple and began to drive out the money changers. Later, Jesus was approached by the religious authorities, and they asked him in Luke 20:2, "***Tell us by what authority You are doing these things, or who is the one who gave You this authority***?" Rather than answer their question directly, Jesus told another parable, but only after He had made it clear that He was no more obliged to answer their questions than they were inclined to answer His. At this point, Jesus addressed the crowd, not the religious authorities, by telling the parable of the vine-growers.

We need to be careful interpreting this parable because it would be easy to assume that the man who planted the vineyard is Jesus, but that is not the case. Remember that Jesus told this parable to indirectly answer the question asked of Him by the religious authorities, who wanted to know by what authority He was throwing out the moneychangers and teaching in the temple.

In the parable, God the Father is the man who planted a vineyard, the Jewish authorities are the vine-growers, the

Old Testament prophets are the slaves who went to the vine-growers to receive some of the fruit, and Jesus is the Heir. If you look at the parable in this framework you will once again see the picture of Jesus as heir of all things, and in this case Jesus is telling the religious authorities that they are really only share-croppers, who own nothing and have no legitimate claim to anything, yet they deny the true heir what is due Him, and kill Him in the process.

Seen from this framework, the parable answers the question the authorities asked; Jesus's authority comes from God the Father. The answer Jesus gave was complete, accurate, damming, and prophetic. The parallel passage in Matthew 21:33-46 contains an interesting detail that is not included in the Luke passage. Matthew 21:45 reads, "***When the Chief Priests and the Pharisees heard His parables, they understood that He was speaking about them***." Based on this verse, it is clear that the Pharisees understood that in the parable, Jesus positioned Himself as the heir, and them as the vine-growers. Jesus didn't just answer their question, although no one understood what He was doing, He prophesied that they would soon kill Him. In this parable Jesus declared Himself as heir of all things, but He also made the case that His death would be a wrongful, grievous, and unjustified murder.

Below is a chart that points out the differences in the three parables we looked at.

- Matthew 25:14-30
  - Master goes on a journey.
  - Gives Talents to three servants.
  - Five talents to one servant – Invested earned five talents.

- Two talents to one servant – Invested earned four talents.
- One talent to the last servant – Buried, earned nothing.
- The talent from the servant with one talent was given to the servant with 10 talents.
- Servant with one talent cast out.

- Luke 19:11-27
    - A nobleman went to a distant country to receive a Kingdom.
    - Gave ten slaves one mina each.
    - One slave took his mina and earned an additional 10 minas.
    - One slave took his mina and earned an additional 5 minas.
    - One slave took his mina and kept it in a handkerchief and earned nothing.
    - The mina from the last slave was taken and given to the first one.

- Luke 20:9-18
    - Man planted a vineyard and rented it out to vine-growers.
    - The first slave the man sent to collect some of the fruit was beaten and thrown out.
    - The second slave was also beaten and thrown out.
    - The third slave was beaten and thrown out.
    - Next, the man sent his son, the heir, and they killed him.
    - The man had the vinedressers killed and gave the vineyard to others.

At this point I want to draw our attention to an important distinction between the two genealogies of Jesus featured in the gospel of Matthew and the gospel of Luke, which further demonstrate the concept of Jesus as the heir. If you have ever studied those genealogies, you might have come to the conclusion that there is a contradiction between Matthew's gospel and Luke's, but I want us to revisit those genealogies for a moment.

Genealogies of Jesus

Matthew	Luke
Abraham	Abraham
Issac	Isaac
Jacob	Jacob
Judah	Judah
Perez	Perez
Herzon	Hezron
Ram	Ram
Abinadab	Admin
Nashon	Amminadab
Salmon	Nashon
Boaz	Salmon
Obed	Boaz
Jesse	Obed
David	Jesse
Solomon	David
Rehaboam	Nathan
Abijam	Mattatha
Asa	Menna
Jehosephat	Melea
Joram	Eliakim
Azaria	
(Uzziam)	Jonam
Jotham	Joseph
Ahaz	Judah
Hezzekiah	Simeon
Mennaseh	Levi
Amon	Matthat
Josiah	Jorim
Jeconiah	Eliezer
Sheiteal	Joshua
Zerrubbable	Er
Abiud	Elmadam
Eliakim	Cosam

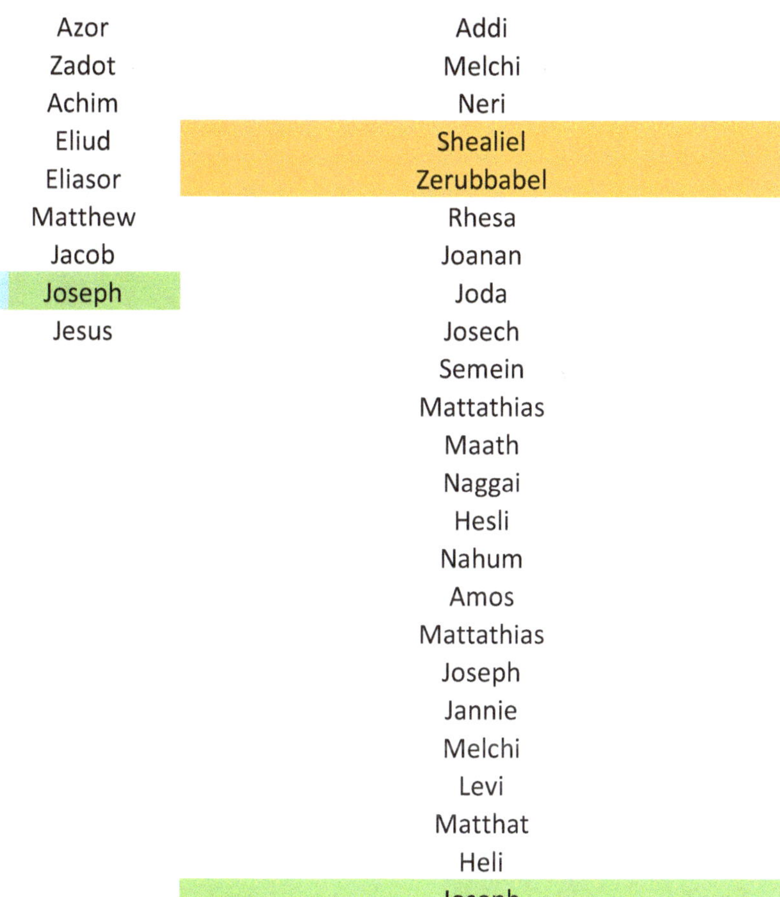

Jesus

Two Genealogies of Jesus

Each of the four gospels looks at Jesus with a different emphasis. Matthew emphasizes Jesus as the Jewish Messiah,

Mark emphasizes Jesus the suffering servant, Luke emphasizes the humanity of Jesus, and John emphasizes the deity of Jesus. Both Matthew and Luke contain genealogies of Jesus, but Matthew traces Jesus back to Abraham, who was the first Jew, while Luke traces Jesus back to Adam, who was the first human.

As Christians we affirm that the Bible is the inerrant and authoritative Word of God. Because the Bible is inerrant in its original manuscripts we must read it with an understanding that when we come across passages that are difficult to understand, or are difficult to reconcile with other sections of the Bible, rather than assume there is a contradiction or an error in the text, we dig deeper to better understand why we are struggling with the passage. In addition, with an awareness of our human limitations we prayerfully seek understanding from the Holy Spirit. We also avail ourselves of help offered by centuries of theologians, biblical scholars, commentators, and apologists.

While some people believe both genealogies represent the line of Mary, others believe both genealogies represent the line of her husband, Joseph. Because we can stipulate that both Mary and Joseph came from Adam, and we can further stipulate that both Mary and Joseph were Hebrews, let's begin our examination of the two genealogies at Abraham. Beginning with Abraham and moving forward, the first divergence we see in the line comes after Ram, the son of Hezron. This does not present a problem because we know that Hebrew prophecy agrees that the Messiah would come through the line of Judah, who precedes Ram in both genealogies by three generations (Judah, Perez, Hezron, Ram). Although we can see that both lines do emerge from Judah, this leaves us with our first problem.

If both genealogies focus solely on Mary's husband Joseph, why is there a divergence between the two lines from Ram through David, and then from David to Joseph? Whether the line is that of Mary or that of Joseph, we read in the Hebrew Prophesy that the Messiah will be a descendant of David, so why isn't there consistency in the line from Ram through David? Another significant divergence occurs after David, where Matthew continues along the line of David's son Solomon, and Luke continues along the line of David's son Nathan.

Rather than try to walk through all the hermeneutical gymnastics to explain the most popular explanations for the two genealogies, I encourage you to conduct a study of these genealogies on your own, but I will briefly touch on a few possibilities and identify the one that I believe makes the most sense.

Liz Abrams wrote a very insightful article in the December 23, 2022, edition of Answers in Genesis, an online service that can be found at www.answersingenesis.org. In her article, Abrams goes into considerable depth to explain the differences between the genealogies in Matthew and Luke. In summary, Abrams believes that both genealogies are Joseph's because all biblical genealogies are patrilineal. She believes that the genealogy in Luke traces Joseph's lineage as an adopted son of Heli, the father of his wife, Mary, while the genealogy in Matthew traces Joseph's biological lineage through his biological father, Jacob.

Zondervan has published a very helpful article on their ZA Blog dated December 14, 2016, titled, "Why are Jesus' genealogies in Matthew and Luke Different?" In this blog, three possible theories for the differences are proposed:

1. One genealogy is Mary's while the other is Joseph's.
    a. In this theory, the genealogy in Matthew traces the lineage of Joseph, while the genealogy in Luke traces the lineage of Mary.
2. One genealogy is a royal genealogy, and the other is a physical genealogy.
    a. In this theory, Matthew, who is writing for a Jewish audience, traces the royal lineage of Jesus through Joseph back to David through the Kings of Judah. Luke traces the lineage of Mary back to Adam, which gives us the physical lineage of Jesus back to the original man.
3. Joseph had two fathers. (Levirate Marriage)
    a. This theory suggests that both Heli (Luke's gospel) and Jacob (Matthew's gospel) were brothers, possibly even half-brothers. When one brother died, it fell to the surviving brother to marry his deceased brother's widow to raise an heir for him. Therefore, both genealogies are Joseph's, one through his biological father and the other through his biological father's brother.

As much as I like the third option above, I find the Levirate marriage theory, as explained in Deuteronomy 25:5, does not adequately explain the divergence in the two lines because it does not resolve a crucial problem. If both Heli and Jacob were, in one sense or another, fathers of Joseph, one would expect both Heli and Jacob to have had the same father, even if they had different mothers. Therefore, the lineage moving backward, through the father of both men, should be identical beginning with their father, but these two lines are not identical. Further, we see more generations between

David and Joseph in Luke's gospel than we see in Matthew's. With that said, I am inclined to view the explanation offered by Abrams as the more plausible alternative.

Abrams suggests that the genealogy in Matthew's gospel is the biological lineage of Joseph, and the genealogy in Luke is Mary's biological lineage. However, she suggests that Mary's father was Heli and that he had no sons of his own. Therefore, Heli adopted Joseph, which was a fairly common practice, and this adoption would have entitled Mary to whatever Heli possessed because she was betrothed to Heli's adopted son Joseph.

The reason I prefer Abram's explanation is because it demonstrates that whether one traces the lineage of Jesus through His adoptive father Heli or through his biological father Jacob, the birth of Jesus affirms His lineage, humanly speaking, back to Abraham, through Judah and through David, because Mary was His mother. I say humanly speaking because as Christians, we affirm the immaculate conception, meaning that Jesus had only one human parent, and that was Mary.

There is more to like about this explanation. Abrams' explanation makes Jesus the heir of all things through His divine nature as the Son of God, and it perpetuates the theme of Jesus as the heir humanly. According to Hebrew prophesy Jesus's adoption affirms His status as heir through Joseph. The adoptions of Jesus by Joseph and that of Joseph by Heli are strong, binding, legal covenants within the Jewish tradition, and these adoptions give us a picture of the strength and significance of our spiritual adoption as co-heirs with Jesus. With this in mind, it is no surprise that as we begin to look at the next facet, Jesus as God, we turn first to the Gospel of John.

Chapter Two

Jesus as God

In his gospel, John refers to Jesus as The Word, and there is such an incredible amount of theology packed into just the first three verses of his gospel. "***In the beginning was the Word, and the Word was with God, and the Word was God. He was in the beginning with God. All things came into being through Him, and apart from Him nothing came into being that has come into being***." (John 1:1-3) In these first three verses of John's gospel, we get our theology of:

- **Jesus as eternal** – Like God the Father, Jesus exists outside of time. "***In the beginning was the Word.***"
- **Jesus as God** – Jesus is coequal with God; He is the second member of the Trinity. "**The Word was God.**"
- **Jesus as creator** – The creation narrative in Genesis 1 and 2 depicts God as being at work through the agency of Jesus. "***All things came into being through Him, and apart from Him nothing came into being that has come into being***".

The question for us in this study is: what did John experience during the years he spent with Jesus which led him to conclude that much of what he had previously attributed to God the Father alone was a shared attribute of His Son, Jesus? Certainly, John wrote under the influence of the Holy Spirit, but as he reflected on his time with Jesus, he concluded that he had spent those years walking with the living God. As John sat in exile on the island of Patmos, preparing to write his gospel, what were the events that led him to this epiphany?

Wine, Wedding, and Witnessing the Divine (John 2:1-12)

Among the four gospels, John paints the definitive portrait of the deity of Jesus. The opening words of John's gospel compel us to believe that Jesus is one with and equal to God the Father. "***In the beginning was the Word [Jesus] and the Word was with God, and the Word was God. He was in the beginning with God. All things came into being through Him, and apart from Him nothing came into being that has come into being. In Him was life, and the life was the Light of men.***" (John 1:1-4) John goes on in verse 14 to describe the transcendence of Jesus, becoming flesh and dwelling among us.

The entire thrust of John's gospel is to declare the deity of Jesus and to draw us into a state of believing in Jesus. After working through the deity and transcendence of Jesus, John describes the work of John the Baptist in preparing the way for Jesus, and then he pivots to the start of Jesus's earthly ministry and calling His disciples. I mention all of this because it is a very fast progression from Jesus being baptized by John, calling His disciples, and then in chapter two, we see the first of many miracles, which began at the wedding in Cana.

For the first demonstration of His divine attributes, Jesus chose the setting of a wedding, and He did something unprecedented. Although we have Old Testament miracles involving healing and raising the dead, until the wedding at Cana, no one had ever transformed one substance (Water) into another substance (Wine). But that is what Jesus did when He transformed water into wine. I do not want us to make too much of the symbolism involved in what occurred, but I also do not want us to miss something significant. A marriage involves God miraculously making one flesh out of two. (Matthew 19:5) For the couple being married, this was the celebration of a new beginning. The wine ran out, and the only one at the wedding who could miraculously address the problem created wine out of a substance that cannot naturally, let alone spontaneously, transform into wine.

Of all the miracles in the Bible, I had always thought this first miracle of Jesus did not compare with miracles like bringing a dead person back to life, expelling demons, commanding the sea to be calm, or feeding the multitudes. I think it is safe to say that my lack of understanding about how wine is made kept me from fully appreciating this first miracle of Jesus, which in some respects may have been His most spectacular. In order to better understand what Jesus did during the wedding at Cana, I had to study the wine-making process a little. After gaining some understanding of how wine is typically made, I thought about how those who were at the wedding and knew what Jesus had done would have reacted to what they knew and what they saw.

Jesus lived in a wine culture. During the time when Jesus was on earth, beverage choices were very limited. People drank water, milk, a limited amount of tea, and wine. Everyone understood that making wine was a process without shortcuts. The head waiter did not know that the wine brought to him by the servants was water just moments prior to him tasting it. To the head waiter the only thing unusual about the wine was the fact that it was the best of the wine served that day and rather than bringing it out at the beginning of the wedding as most people would have done, this premium wine had been brought out to be served at a time when most of the guests would have been intoxicated enough that they would not have noticed or minded if the host had served them the inferior wine. By contrast, the servants, the disciples, and Mary were fully aware that something miraculous had occurred.

Before we go any deeper into our application of this story, I want to offer a way of thinking about miracles. Webster's online dictionary defines a miracle as "An extraordinary event manifesting divine intervention in human affairs." I find that definition helpful, but I want to offer a working definition for our study, which goes a step further, and I think as we move through this book, we will find that the definition I am offering will apply to every event commonly referred to as a miracle. Therefore, I submit that *a miracle is a temporary suspension of the laws of physics*.

Our interest in the wedding at Cana centers around how those who knew what had happened would have responded to the event. Present at the wedding were Peter, his brother Andrew, Philip, Nathaneal, Mary the mother of Jesus, and Jesus's brothers, presumably James and Jude. Each of these people was aware that Jesus had told the servants to fill up the vessels with water, and they each knew those servants had taken these large vessels to the head waiter, who drew some of the liquid from the vessels, tasted it, and discovered that it was not only wine, but the best of wines.

In my brief study of the wine-making process, I discovered a few things that really bring this story to life. Jesus used that which is useless for wine making in order to make wine. Jesus neither had nor did He use anything that would have been necessary for making wine. Nothing I have read about wine-making indicates that water is ever used in the wine-making process, yet Jesus began with water, which is a useless substance in the wine-making process. Materially speaking, wine making requires grapes, and it can involve other substances like clay, eggs, or sugar. The other thing wine making requires in abundance that Jesus did not have was time. Put another way, Jesus had an abundance of what He did not need, [Water], and nothing that He did need in order to make wine. This suspension of the laws of physics is what gives us the miracle.

Although techniques vary depending on the type of wine being made, the flavors sought, whether the wine will be white, red, or rosé, and whether the winemaker is using an antiquated or modern process, wine making involves the following basic steps:

1. Harvesting
2. Crushing/Pressing
3. Fermentation
4. Clarification
5. Bottling and Aging

Without any instruction or training, we can all look at the above 5 steps and see the impossibility of transforming water, which is a useless substance in the wine-making process, into wine within the brief moments Jesus had to perform this miracle. Looking at the above list, we can see that each of these steps takes considerable time.

- **Harvesting** grapes in the first century would have taken teams of people several hours to acquire enough material for even one of the six water pots, which contained 20-30 gallons.
- **Crushing** grapes in the first century would have taken teams of people several hours. Crushing enough grapes to fill just one of the water pots with enough raw material would have taken the better part of another day.

- **Fermentation** time depends on several factors, but it cannot be rushed. Once the crushed grapes have been set aside for fermentation, it would have taken weeks before the crushed grapes would have successfully fermented, even for a low alcohol content.
- **Clarification** is a tedious process of separating the unwanted grape skins and seeds from the fermented juice of the grapes.
- **Bottling and aging** for what the head waiter called "Good Wine" would have taken several months.

This is what makes our definition of a miracle valuable. What Jesus did in that moment was to suspend the laws of physics by taking water, a simple, uncomplex substance that is not used in making wine, and create from it a very complex substance like wine within seconds. The laws of physics simply will not allow water to become wine under any circumstances. Water lacks all of the physical properties necessary for wine to be created. Further, the laws of physics will permit grapes to transform into wine, but only through a complex and time-consuming process. Suspending the laws of physics, Jesus created wine, bypassing the harvesting, crushing, fermenting, clarifying, and aging required for transforming grapes into wine. In total, these steps take months to complete, but Jesus suspended the laws of physics which govern wine making, and He made not just wine, but good wine in a matter of seconds.

When we consider the question of how the mother and the companions of Jesus might have responded to what they saw within the context of what they knew, we can reasonably assume they had never seen anything like this before. It is also reasonable to assume that even if none of them had ever made wine themselves, they would have known that wine does not come from water, it comes from grapes, and that it takes more than the will of an ordinary man and a few seconds to produce wine, even if one had grapes. However, as we already mentioned, Jesus did not have grapes, and He did not have months to invest in creating the wine. Therefore, we can reasonably conclude that everyone who knew what had happened was faced with the certainty that the laws of physics had been suspended in this case, and that the cause of this suspension was none other than Jesus. Armed with this set of facts, the disciples and Mary would have believed a miracle had just been done in their presence, and they would have seen it as an act of God.

What's In a Name? (John 8:58)

More than any of the other three gospel writers, John focuses on Jesus as God, the second member of the Trinity. In the first three verses of his gospel, John tells us that Jesus existed in the beginning of time with God the Father and that He was directly involved in creating the world. We will look at the shocking statement Jesus made in John 8:58, but the context of this verse involves an important exchange between Jesus and the religious authorities at the beginning of the chapter. The encounter is recorded in John 8:1-12, and it began when the Scribes and Pharisees brought a woman caught in adultery to Jesus, and they expected to trip Jesus up by forcing Him to either defend her behavior or condemn her. When their attempts to trap Jesus failed, and He turned their hypocrisy back on them, they continued to challenge Him. Starting in John 8:12, Jesus methodically developed the case for His own deity using the very laws and scriptures they held up as a standard.

In this confrontation, Jesus even accused the assembled Jews of being sons of Satan. Along the way, Jesus made the statement, "***Your father Abraham rejoiced to see My day, and he saw it and was glad.***" In that statement, Jesus was tying them to the scriptures and saying that if, in fact, they are truly Jews, they should rejoice over whatever Abraham, the father of the Jews, rejoiced over. This is where Jesus sprang His trap. Their response was perfectly reasonable and predictable. Jesus said that Abraham rejoiced to see His day, so the Jews asked how that could be when Abraham had been dead by then for centuries. The only way Abraham could have seen Jesus is if Jesus was over 1,500 years old, or if He was God.

There were many charismatic rabbis in the first century, but none of them made the claims that Jesus made. One of the distinguishing characteristics of Jesus was His claim of being equal to God. Jesus did not make this claim by simply saying He was God; Jesus made his claim by demonstrating through scripture and through His behavior that He is God. In this instance, Jesus identified himself with an ancient name for God, which was well known to the spiritual leaders of that day.

When Moses stood before the burning bush asking God who he should tell the Hebrews had sent him, God said, "***Tell them I am sent you***." (Exodus 3:14) In this conversation with the Jews, Jesus used the name "I Am" in an extraordinary way. When the Jews said to Jesus, "***You are not yet fifty years old, and have You seen Abraham?***" (John 8:57), Jesus said, "***Before Abraham was born, I am***."

If Jesus were merely trying to point out that He is ancient, he could have said, before Abraham was born, I was born. However, that is not what Jesus said, and that is not what He intended to say. Jesus did this in such a way that everyone knew exactly what He was doing. It is not readily apparent from the English text, but Jesus actually doubled down on his claim of deity.

If a person wanted to repeat in Greek what Moses wrote in Hebrew, describing the burning bush experience from Exodus 3:14, the person would have used the Greek construction, "Eimi," meaning "I am," or I exist. However, Jesus said, "Ego eimi," which added the emphatic pronoun "ego" that we would translate as "I." When you add the emphatic pronoun, Jesus was saying, "I, I am." If Jesus was only saying He existed back when Abraham was alive, He might have used the imperfect tense of eimi which is "en". This would have been understood as, "I was." However, the construction Jesus used was immediately understood by those who heard Him as a claim to have continuously existed in Abraham's time, before Abraham's time, and presently; this is what made His remark so audacious, because only God could make such a claim. To get the full effect it helps to imagine Jesus standing before the Jews patting His hand on His chest and annunciating each syllable as He said, "Ego eimi," or "I, I am." The effect is Jesus identifying Himself as Yahweh.

Debates and teachings among and between rabbis and religious authorities were common, but everything about the ministry of Jesus was uncommon. The debates held during the first century in and around the temple or synagogues followed certain rules, and there were some lines that just were not crossed. Jesus repeatedly walked up to those lines and crossed them without any concern for whom He might have offended. His ministry and His tone would have been seen as audacious, and those who followed him certainly would have become accustomed to experiencing something out of the ordinary whenever they hung out with Him. Jesus made an intentional practice of defying archaic, unscriptural, and self-serving customs. In this case, Jesus gave everyone something to talk about.

The penalty for any human claiming to be God was death by stoning, and I would imagine that as this confrontation built up to a climax, the tension could be cut with a knife. Those who followed Jesus and knew where He was going with his line of reasoning were probably wondering when He would veer off or back down, but He did neither. Having stayed the course, all of them were surely expecting this would be Jesus's last day of living, but He was not stoned.

The fact that Jesus was not stoned is critical to understanding what those who spent time with and knew Jesus would have experienced and how those experiences shaped their concept of who Jesus was. John 8:59 says, "***Therefore they picked up stones to throw at Him, but Jesus hid himself and went out of the temple***." This verse begs the question, how exactly did Jesus hide himself? One minute Jesus was standing there, telling them about their moral and spiritual deficiencies, claiming to be God, and then the next minute He was hidden from their sight as they picked up stones to kill Him.

This is one of the many reasons you can believe it when Jesus said, "***No one has taken it [My life] away from Me, but I lay it down on My own initiative***." (John 10:18) This is not the only time Jesus did something like this. When Jesus was teaching in Nazareth, He read from Isaiah and proclaimed that He was the fulfillment of that scripture. Ultimately, this situation also ended with the Jews wanting to kill Him, this time by throwing Him off a cliff. However, in this instance, Jesus, with His back to the cliff, simply passed through the crowd without being stopped. (Luke 4:16-30)

As we try to imagine the experience of being at the side of Jesus during this confrontation, or in the crowd that witnessed the exchange between Jesus and the Jews, or even as we imagine what the Jews who confronted Jesus must have thought of this audacious man who claimed to be God, we now must add to the encounter that when the crowd picked up stones to kill Jesus, He vanished from their presence which certainly added to the sense that He was more than human. As you transport yourself back to the 1st century and step into the crowd gathered around Jesus, here is what I encourage you to consider. Stoning a person is intended to be a close, personal, and immediate means of dispensing justice.

For stones to become lethal, they must either be light enough to be hurled at significant velocity, or they must be heavy enough to accomplish the same wounds within closer confines. No one would pick up stones and then go looking for the person they were going to stone. In this case, they were talking to Jesus; they judged His words to be blasphemous, and they planned to execute him immediately. Jesus was, so to speak, right in their crosshairs. For the Jews to accomplish their intended task, Jesus would have had to be close enough to kill, and not in a position to evade His attackers by any natural means, yet Jesus simply vanished.

Jesus's declaration of deity, along with the supernatural evasion of His would-be executioners, would have been extremely dramatic for those in His presence, causing them to be awestruck by Him. For His followers, these incidents would have drawn them closer to Jesus and caused them to want to spend more time with Him. At the same time, these incidents would have deepened the determination of His accusers to kill Him and put a quick end to His growing ministry.

Asleep In The boat

"***And behold, there arose a great storm on the sea, so that the boat was being covered with the waves; but Jesus Himself was asleep. And they came to Him and woke Him, saying, 'Save us, Lord; we are perishing!' He said to them, 'Why are you afraid, you men of little faith?' Then He got up and rebuked the winds and the sea, and it became perfectly calm***" (Matthew 8:24-27). Years ago, I saw a movie called The Perfect Storm. In this movie, there is a scene at the end where a great storm tosses huge modern fishing boats like toys in a bathtub. I think of this scene every time I read Matthew 8:24-27. A tempest arose instantly, and these seasoned, experienced fishermen were terrified, believing they would not survive the next few minutes.

It would not be remarkable for me to be terrified in this situation or one far less dramatic because I cannot swim. Therefore, being surrounded by water is always frightening to me, but to fully appreciate this situation, we have to consider the fact that the men who accompanied Jesus in this boat had spent their entire lives fishing on the open sea, and they had faced perils on the sea multiple times. These men were not easily scared, and it would have taken a storm of great magnitude to frighten them.

There is so much rich theology packed into these four short verses, but I want to remain focused on our study objective which is to insert ourselves into these moments in time when our Lord and Savior walked the earth and conducted His ministry. I find it interesting that His disciples, fearing for their lives, did not wake Jesus to simply to tell Him they were about to die and that all hope was lost, or to give Him a warning so that He could jump overboard and attempt to save His own life. Setting aside for the moment the fact that Jesus was asleep while the boat was being tossed about like a toy in a bathtub, let's examine how the disciples dealt with the situation. The disciples woke Jesus and said, "***Save us, Lord; we are perishing***." There are three significant sections to the phrase they used that are worthy of our examination:

Save us – The disciples were beginning to learn that Jesus had power that other men did not possess. However, there was nothing in their body of experience that would have led them to the conclusion that they could be saved, yet they turned to Jesus and implored Him to do the impossible. Again, let's consider our definition of a miracle: the temporary suspension of the laws of physics. With regard to the sea, these disciples were well acquainted with the laws of physics. As such, they understood that when you are caught in a tempest of this magnitude, the force of the water will eventually overturn the boat, you will be tossed into the sea, and you will die. Therefore, asking Jesus to do that which could not be done naturally is all the more curious. Even if the storm was going to eventually die down, no human could cause this to take place. The laws of physics dictate that wind, and waves do not submit to the vocal commands of a man. However, the disciples fully expected Jesus to do that which could not be done naturally. They were hoping that Jesus could perform a miracle which no one but God could perform. This leads us to the second section of the phrase they used.

Lord – The disciples referred to Jesus as Lord. The word translated as lord in English is Kurios in Greek. Kurios is a title used for someone in power or authority, or someone who is a landowner. We derive our concept of a landlord from this term of reverence and respect, but it is within Christian parlance that we derive our concept of Jesus as our Lord and Savior. As followers of Jesus, we defer to Him as the ultimate authority, the One who purchased, redeemed, and ultimately exercises ownership over our lives. However, Kurios is not the same term sometimes translated in the Old Testament Hebrew as Lord.

The Hebrew word sometimes translated as Lord is Elohim which is a term of deity. Throughout the New Testament, Jesus is referred to as Lord, (Kurios) or as Teacher, (Rabbi), and in this instance, the disciples were not looking for a teacher, they were looking for a leader, they were looking for someone with power and authority, and although they hoped Jesus could save them, they were not yet ready to attribute His power and authority to deity. However, having exhausted all of their own options, they turned to Jesus, hoping He could pull off some sort of miracle that might save them.

They may have hoped Jesus could somehow steady the boat until they could ride out the storm, or that He might offer a suggestion they had not considered, but it never occurred to them that Jesus would or even could calm the waters instantaneously, which is exactly what He did. We know they were not expecting a miracle of this sort because in Matthew 8:27 they said, "***What kind of man is this, that even the winds and the sea obey Him.***" One moment the winds and waves were tossing the boat about, then Jesus said, "***Hush be still***" and instantly the sea was calm. (Mark 4:38-39)

<u>We are perishing</u> – Put another way, the disciples were saying to Jesus, absent some intervention, we are all about to die, including you Jesus. This ought not be confused with desperation or futility, it is more like the disciples, recognizing that they had come to the end of their own resources, had done all they could do, and their salvation was now wholly dependent upon Jesus.

Here's an example of what I mean. I am not mechanically inclined at all. There was a time when I could change the oil on a car and even give a car a tune up, but that was a long time ago. These days the most I can contribute to automotive repair is to pull the credit card from my wallet and hand it to the mechanic. However, I have a brother who is very handy under the hood of a car. If the two of us were driving down a dark country road with no repair shops in sight in the middle of the night and the car broke down with him asleep in the driver's seat, I might look under the hood quickly but then I would wake up my brother. I would probably say something like, the car has broken down, I cannot fix it, there are no repair stations nearby and even if there were one, it's the middle of the night. If we are going to get to where we are going, I need you to do what you do and get this car running because if you don't, we will be stranded here. My point is that the disciples were not saying all hope was lost; they were saying that Jesus was their only hope.

At this point, I want to return to the fact that Jesus was asleep in the boat. The disciples were wide awake, doing everything their years of experience told them was necessary to do in order to survive. Aside from their experience and training, as human beings facing a perilous situation, they were on high alert, and no doubt all the muscles in their bodies were tense. Jesus, on the other hand, was enjoying a peaceful nap, completely unconcerned with the perils which terrified His disciples.

If I were one of the disciples, panicking as I certainly would have been, watching all the other disciples run around frantically, deep within my panicked heart, there would have been some sense of awe within me to see Jesus peacefully at rest in the boat. Absent my panic, I would have desired the peace and calm of the Lord. After watching Jesus calm the sea, I would have longed for Jesus's ability to remain at peace in the midst of such peril, and I am sure witnessing this would have been extremely endearing to His disciples, even before He took action to calm the sea. The question this passage of scripture leaves us with is, who wouldn't want to be around someone like Jesus in the midst of a storm?

Do Not Be Unbelieving But Believing

Many years ago, I spent a considerable amount of time speaking with Jehovah's Witnesses about their religious beliefs. During that season of my life, I had not studied the Bible much, but my goal was to win arguments and prove that my beliefs were right and theirs were wrong. To be honest, I'm not sure I won a single argument with any of them, but feeling defeated and often confused after those discussions did encourage me to be a better student of the scriptures.

Among other things, Jehovah's Witnesses reject the Protestant Christian doctrine of Jesus's deity. It has been decades since I debated any Jehovah's Witness, but I have learned that skepticism should not be dismissed as either ignorance or recalcitrance; it should be embraced with hopefulness. A person who is skeptical is not closed to the truth; they are simply not yet convinced of the truth, and it is our call to lead them to the source of truth rather than try to win arguments through our own persuasiveness.

I wish I knew back then that when it comes to understanding the deity of Christ, a rich source of truth is found in the Gospel of John. The primary focus of John's gospel is to establish and defend the deity of Christ, and to encourage his readers to believe that Jesus is God incarnate. John sets the agenda for his gospel from the very first verse, "***In the beginning was the Word, [Jesus] and the Word was with God, and the Word was God***." (John 1:1) Toward the end of John's gospel, after documenting numerous events, discourses, and miracles which speak to the deity of Jesus, he writes, "***Therefore many other signs Jesus also performed in the presence of the disciples, which are not written in this book; but these have been written so that you may believe that Jesus is the Christ, the Son of God, and that believing, you may have life in His name***." (John 20:31-32)

In this chapter, we are looking at Jesus as God, and there is evidence of this throughout the Bible, beginning with the first chapter of Genesis, which says, "In the beginning God created the heavens and the earth." (Genesis 1:1) In the Gospel of John, we read. "***All things came into being through Him [Jesus], and apart from Him nothing came into being that has come into being***," (John 1:3). We also see what theologians call Christophanies in the Old Testament, where Jesus appears to Abraham in Genesis 18, and to Jacob in Genesis 32:24-32. The fact is that evidence for the deity of Christ can be found throughout the Bible from the Old Testament to the New Testament.

One of the disciples, called Thomas, is often referred to as doubting Thomas, but I think the more accurate description of Thomas is that he was a skeptic. Thomas was not one who refused to believe; he was simply unwilling to believe by faith. Thomas's ability to believe was based upon evidence, and before we shake our heads and roll our pious Christian eyes at Thomas, we need some context. The execution of

Jesus was public, and there was no doubt that He had been crucified, hung on the cross, and that he eventually died. These were the facts that Thomas had before him. After three days, Jesus rose from the dead, and He appeared to Mary Magdalene. When Mary reported what she had seen, Peter and John went to the tomb and found it empty. In another instance, Jesus appeared to the other disciples as they gathered behind closed doors. Thomas had heard all of these stories, but he himself had not seen the risen Lord.

Based upon the information Thomas had available to him, he found insufficient evidence to believe that Jesus was alive. Therefore, Thomas said, "***Unless I see in His hands the imprint of the nails, and put my finger into the place of the nails, and put my hand into His side, I will not believe***." (John 20:1-25) Thomas's belief was conditional, so Jesus met those conditions for Thomas. As followers of Jesus, we are now expected to believe and to walk by faith. "***And without faith it is impossible to please Him, for he who comes to God must believe that He is and that He is a rewarder of those who seek him***." (Hebrews 11:6)

We know that faith, by definition, is believing without evidence. "***Now faith is the substance of things hoped for, the evidence of things not seen.***" (Hebrews 11:1) Another way to read Hebrews 11:1 is to say that faith is belief in the existence of things we hope for without seeing them with our human eyes; faith stands in substitution for the things we cannot see. Despite his lack of faith, Thomas was given an extra dispensation of grace by Jesus in this incredible moment because in the days following His resurrection, Jesus revealed Himself to His follower's multiple times for the purpose of building, proliferating, and perpetuating faith among them.

Eight days after Thomas made his declaration not to believe without proof, Jesus made another dramatic appearance, and it was Thomas who instantly connected the dots and realized that they were not only seeing Jesus as their risen Lord (Kurios), they were seeing Jesus as God Himself, in the flesh. After placing his fingers into the nail holes and placing his hands into Jesus's side, Thomas's response was, "***My Lord and my God***!" (John 20:28). With this utterance, Thomas affirmed Jesus as Lord (Kurios) and God (Theos). Every aspect of this appearance by Jesus demands our full attention, and the impact it had on the entire group assembled cannot be overstated. Let's return to our definition of a miracle, the temporary suspension of the laws of physics. I want us to consider two physical realities involved in this appearance of Jesus:

1. **Physical limitations of death** – The laws of physics dictate that only a living human being can move on his/her own volition or speak with other human beings, but the laws of physics had already rendered Jesus dead following a brutal torture and being nailed to the cross.
2. **Physical reality of solid mass** – The laws of physics dictate that solid object "A" cannot pass through solid object "B" without disturbing, disbursing, or displacing solid object "B". The scripture says, "***After eight days His disciples were again inside, and Thomas with them. Jesus came, the doors having been shut, and stood in their midst***." (John 20:26) According to the laws of physics, in order for Jesus to enter the room the door would have to be opened, removed, or an opening would have had to be made in the door, but none of those things occurred. Jesus simply passed through the solid door,

> leaving the door undisturbed and He stood in their midst.

I have found that when reading the Bible, if you are open to it, you will find an abundance of humor. I know we tend to think of Jesus as a very serious person on a serious mission, and He was all of that, but reading scripture I get the impression that Jesus liked to have fun with His disciples. In this situation, the disciples were gathered behind closed doors. The tension during the days following Jesus's crucifixion was heightened by the fact that His body was missing, and the religious authorities wanted to suppress any talk of resurrection, so gatherings such as this would have been very dangerous and very secretive.

There they were behind closed doors probably discussing Jesus secretly in hushed tones, and then suddenly Jesus appeared among them. I imagine them all being in shock at seeing Jesus, who was supposed to be dead, standing in their midst, even though the door was securely shut. While the disciples stood frozen with their mouths wide open, no doubt scared out of their wits at this sudden appearance of Jesus, His first words were, "***Peace be with you***." I guess He could have just said, "Boo!" I doubt peace was their initial reaction to seeing Jesus standing among them. Luke describes the same incident by writing, "***But they were startled and frightened and thought that they were seeing a spirit***." (Luke 24:37) The reaction of His disciples must have been hilarious, and I imagine Jesus got a good laugh out of seeing the expressions on their faces.

Lunch With A Few Close Friends

One of the things I find most endearing about Jesus is not just the miracles He performed, but the nature of those miracles. Jesus tended to go far out of His way with the miracles He performed to leave no doubt that He was doing the impossible. So far in this chapter, we have looked at:

- The wedding at Cana, where Jesus took water and made wine
- Jesus calming a raging storm that threatened to capsize the fishing boat He slept in
- Jesus rising from the dead after being flogged and nailed to a cross
- Jesus passing through a solid door and speaking to His disciples

There are many more miracles we could look at where Jesus goes way beyond to demonstrate the impossibility of what He was doing, like raising Lazarus after he was intombed for four days, or healing the centurion's daughter, or another centurion's servant. In each of these miracles, Jesus actually shows off, and I do not use the term "showing off" irreverently, nor am I saying that Jesus showed off in a human, prideful sense; I mean, Jesus went way above and beyond to demonstrate that He is the image of the invisible God. (Colossians 1:15)

One of Jesus's best-known miracles is the feeding of 5,000 and then the feeding of 4,000. These two miracles were so powerful in part because they were performed in front of such a huge crowd of people. One of the main apologetic arguments for the authenticity of the Bible is that the New Testament was written so very close to the time that Jesus walked the earth. We tend to find value in evidence that is gathered contemporaneously with the events the evidence attests to.

For example, shortly after Donald J Trump was elected as the 43rd President of the United States, he fired FBI director

James Comey. In subsequent interviews, during the investigation led by Robert Mueller, former director Comey made numerous references to "Contemporaneous Notes" he had taken of his conversations with the new president while he was director. These notes were considered to have increased evidentiary value because they were created as the events written about took place.

In the same sense, the authenticity of the Bible is enhanced by the fact that writers such as the Apostle John wrote about Jesus feeding 5,000 and then 4,000 within a relatively short time after the events took place. Because John's gospel was written so close to the time the miracles took place, it gave those who were alleged to be involved in the incident an opportunity to refute those events if they found fault with what he recorded in his gospel. However, there is no record that any of the 9,000 people who ate the meals provided by Jesus refuted the story recorded in John's gospel.

This is not a book on apologetics, and the goal of this book is not to defend the Christian faith, but as we consider the impact Jesus had on the people He interacted with during His time on earth, it is worth noting that the Gospel of John was written within 60 years of the crucifixion of Jesus. If the gospel writers were making these stories up and there was no truth in them, one would think that at least a few of the 9,000 people who were supposed to have been present at the two feedings but left hungry would have called out the gospel writers as liars.

The miracle of Jesus feeding 5,000 and then 4,000 is another example of Him showing off and demonstrating the impossibility of His actions apart from deity. To feed 20 people, or even 100 people with such a small amount of food would have been impressive, but Jesus went way beyond by feeding 5,000 in one event, and then an additional 4,000 at another event. Jesus feeding 5,000 is recorded in all four gospels, but the feeding of 4,000 is only recorded in the gospels of Matthew and Mark, not in Luke or John.

I want to draw your attention to the context in which the feeding of 5,000 took place. Whenever we study scripture, having an awareness of context is imperative. Scriptures taken out of context can give us messages that were never intended, but another danger is that taking scriptures out of context can cause us to miss the messages the scriptures were intended to convey. With regard to Jesus feeding the 5,000, it is very helpful to consider what was taking place when Jesus performed this miracle. We get a significant clue as to what was taking place from the first three words of John 6:1 which read, "***After these things***." With this in mind, we must consider what "***Things***" preceded the miracle. Jesus feeding the 5,000 was the culmination of events which began back in John 5:1 where Jesus healed the man at the pool of Bethesda.

People went to the pool of Bethesda to be healed, and this man was so afflicted that he could not get into the pool by himself. Making matters worse, the man had no one to put him into the pool when the angel stirred up the water. Jesus healed the man without him having to get into the pool, but as usual, Jesus performed this miracle on the Sabbath, which sparked another contentious debate between Jesus and the religious authorities.

During the debate between Jesus and the religious authorities, Jesus made some of His most powerful claims of deity by claiming to be the Son of God, and equal with God. (John 5) In John 5:18 we read, "***For this reason*** [Verse 17], ***therefore the Jews were seeking all the more to kill Him,***

***because He not only was breaking the Sabath, but also was calling God His own Father, making Himself equal with God.*"** Jesus's rebuke of the religious authorities continues from John 5:19 through John 5:47. When the story picks up at John 6:1 Jesus had ceased His rebuke of the Jews, but the crowd had witnessed Him healing the sick, including the man at the pool of Bethesda. Jesus had been showing off, and the crowd was looking for a show. (John 6:2) As we return to our definition of a miracle, *the temporary suspension of the laws of physics*, I want to take a look at the laws of physics which were suspended in feeding 5,000 and then 4,000 people.

1. **The physical laws of weights and measures** – The number of people in the first instance was 5,000 and then later Jesus fed 4,000 people. In order to be satiated, a hungry first century Jew could probably consume one half pound of fish along with about a six-inch square of barley bread (one barley loaf). Therefore, in order for each man among the crowd of 5,000 to be satiated the disciples would have needed to provide about 2,500 pounds of fish, and about 5,000 loaves of barley bread. Scripture does not tell us what kind of fish the boy whom Andrew found among the crowd had, (John 6:8-9). However, some of the fish common to that region during the first century were perch, sea bass, tilapia, and a few other varieties. The average perch weighs about 2.5 pounds, the average tilapia weighs about 2.4 pounds, and the average sea bass weighs about 5.2 pounds. Let's say the boy Andrew found had two average sea bass, which would mean the disciples would have had about 10.5 pounds of fish to feed 5,000 men. This would mean that each man would receive an equal

portion amounting to about 0.0021 pounds of fish; an amount that would fit neatly atop a pencil eraser. Philip's response to Jesus makes so much more sense with this in mind. Philip said to Jesus, "***Two hundred denarii worth of bread is not sufficient for them, for everyone to receive a little.***" Two hundred denarii worth of bread would have been about seven months wages which is a fraction of what it would have cost to purchase 2,500 pounds of fish and 5,000 loaves of bread, yet Jesus produced this staggering amount of food within a few minutes.

2. **The physical laws of math** – If we can assume that each basket used to take up the extra fragments of bread and fish could hold three fish and six loaves of bread, after everyone had eaten their fill of fish and bread, the disciples would have collected 36 fish and 72 loaves. The laws of mathematics dictate that one cannot end with more than one begins with absent some means of reproduction. A person can certainly start with two living fish and eventually end up with over 2,500 pounds of fish, if the person begins with one living male fish and one living female fish, and the person has sufficient time and conditions for procreation to result in exponential growth. However, it is physically impossible to begin with two dead fish and within moments end up with 2,500 pounds of fish that are prepared for human consumption.

As the disciples distributed the fish and the loaves, the food multiplied. Again, this is Jesus showing off and outdoing even the Old Testament prophet Elisha, who instructed a widow to take the small amount of

> oil she had and pour it into as many large vessels as she could gather. Following Elisha's instructions, the woman gathered several vessels and was able to pour the small amount of oil out filling as many large vessels as were able to fit into her home. (2 Kings 4:1-7) As amazing as Elisha's miracle was, it does not compare to the mathematical magnitude of what Jesus did with two fish and five loaves of bread. What's more incredible is that Jesus fed 5,000 with 2 fish and 5 loaves, but then He fed 4,000 with 7 loaves and a few small fish. Therefore, Jesus fed more people with 2 fish and 5 loaves that He fed with 7 loaves and several, (more than two) fish. (Matthew 15:32-38)

It has been argued by Bible scholars that the number of people fed were likely much higher than 5,000 and then 4,000 because it would be common for women and children to have been excluded from the count. For simplicity's sake, I took the numbers strictly as they are written because the enormity of what Jesus did remains within the realm of the impossible whether we are talking about 5,000 men, women, and children, or the number swells to 20,000 by adding an average of one woman and two children for every man gathered.

Although most of the people in the crowd may not have initially known that Jesus started with only 2 fish and 5 loaves, or in the case of feeding the 4,000 He started with 7 loaves and several fish, all of the disciples in Jesus's inner circle would have known, and perhaps hundreds of those who sat near to Jesus as He blessed the food. Those sitting near as Jesus blessed the food and instructed the disciples to distribute it would have known that Jesus's instructions made no sense because 5,000 people cannot be fed with 2 fish and 5 loaves. It is also more than likely that those same people who saw Him bless the food and then send the disciples out to distribute it would have spread the word quickly to those deeper within the crowd that the food they were consuming was the product of another miracle.

One of the cornerstones of my ministry is to draw people, both believers and non-believers into reading the Bible. As followers of the Lord Jesus Christ, I believe we ought to develop a daily routine of reading the Bible. That said, I am also aware that all of us can become so familiar with the stories of miraculous events recorded in the Bible that we cease to be amazed by what we are reading. I also believe that we can fall into the mindset of filtering what we read through our 21st century, western mindset, and this is often where we lose our awe of Jesus and the multiple events in the Bible which, if viewed within the context and setting where and when these events occurred, can leave us totally awestruck.

The crowds of people who ate the food which was provided miraculously by Jesus had heard the stories of miracles performed in the Old Testament by Moses, Joshua, Gideon, Samson, Samuel, Elijah, Elisha, and others, but by the time Jesus arrived, they were awaiting the promised messiah after a 400-year intertestamental period where God had been silent. The people gathered at the feeding of 5,000 and the feeding of 4,000 were not just hungry for food, they were hungry for a fresh revelation of the power of God. They followed Jesus expecting to be awestruck, expecting to see something powerful. As the disciples received from the hand of Jesus a meager portion of food, and began to walk toward the crowd they must have been thinking, "*What has Jesus gotten us into now? These people are going to stone us as we present each of them with barely enough food to fit on the tip of a thin twig.*" Then, as they passed out the food it multiplied, and they distributed huge portions to each person in the crowd. Those serving, and those being served would have been absolutely astounded and enamored with the power of God as manifest in His Son, Jesus, the God-Man.

Each of the miracles discussed in this chapter along with the many miracles witnessed by those who walked with Jesus would have continually added to their belief that Jesus was much more than a man, He was in fact Immanual, God among us. If we read the scriptures expecting to be astounded by the works of Jesus, if we suspend our 21st century, western perspective, and adopt the perspective of a 1st century Jew, we too will be amazed at our Lord and Savior. We cannot allow ourselves to continue to read the Bible as some mundane, or even academic exercise used to increase our knowledge and our capacity to argue a point of view. These are not just a collection of stories written to make us feel good or to offer some guidance on how to manage the circumstances of our lives, these are not written merely to show us how to govern our churches, and they are not just fodder for our Sunday sermons either. God has preserved these biblical narratives so that we can step into the past and be raptured, amazed, awestruck, and convinced, that Jesus is God.

The Making Of An Apostle

Although John honed in on the divine attributes of Jesus more narrowly than the other gospel writers, we must broaden our lens a bit if we want to discover how those who spent time with Jesus experienced His divine attributes while they were in His presence. With this in mind, I want to consider the Apostle Paul, who was one of the last Apostles to spend time with Jesus as the risen Lord as opposed to the incarnate Jesus who walked the earth for over 33 ½ years. Of course, John spent time with Jesus as he was exiled on Patmos, writing Revelation, but Paul's encounter with Jesus was so much different than the encounter anyone else had with Him. The many disciples of Jesus, including those in His inner circle, and the religious authorities witnessed Jesus performing miracles such as raising the dead, healing the lame, and giving sight to the blind. However, Paul was the only one who experienced Jesus taking away his vision and then restoring it. Paul was such a zealot, so convinced his persecution of "The Way" was righteous, that Jesus's introduction to Paul had to be powerful, personal, profound, dramatic, and unique. (Acts 9:1-16)

We are first introduced to Paul in Acts 7:58 when he was still Saul, the pharisee from Tarsus who was making a name for himself as a zealous defender of the religious status quo. As such, Saul sought out followers of the sect referred to at that time as, "The Way"' later identified as Christians. During the early days of the church, it became important to define roles within the ministry to ensure that all the needs of the new church were met. It was decided that seven men would be chosen to meet the immediate needs of food distribution and other ministerial duties. These seven men would have been considered deacons, or servants, and among the seven was a man named Stephan who is described in scripture as being full of faith and of the Holy Spirit. (Acts 6:1-8)

As a Spirit-filled believer Stephan began performing great wonders and signs among the people and this caught the attention of some men from what was called the Synagogue of the Freedmen, and these men began to challenge Stephen.

Eventually, the clarity and truth of Stephan's words was so overpowering and convincing, it caused his challengers to stir up false witnesses for the purpose of discrediting him. These men brought Stephan before the high priests who also questioned him. The high priests and Pharisees like Saul liked things the way they were, and they did not want a new sect to rise up and usurp their authority.

It is easy to forget that the Book of Acts, is actually the Acts of the Apostles. Absent a focus on the work of the apostles we can lose sight of who wrote the book, why this book was written, and who or better yet, what the book is written about. The who, why, and what, of Acts has an important impact on the theme of *this* book. We are interested in knowing how those who spent time with Jesus were affected by Him, and The Book of Acts describes in significant detail what happened to them, as a result of spending time with Him. It's somewhat like asking why someone climbed the mountain and learning that they climbed the mountain because they believed there was a treasure buried at the mountain's summit. The gospels help us understand what motivated the apostles, and Acts tells us what the apostles did as a result of being so motivated. Therefore, let's return our attention to the three questions, who, why, and what. The answer to these questions can be found in the first four verses of the first chapter of Luke.

The Book of Acts was written by Luke, and it is a continuation of the gospel he wrote. "***The first account I composed, Theophilus, about all that Jesus began to do and teach until the day when He was taken up to leave, after He had by the Holy Spirit given orders to the apostles whom He had chosen.***" (Acts 1:1-2). The answer to why Luke wrote Acts is the same as his reason for writing the

Gospel of Luke, "***It seemed fitting for me as well, having investigated everything carefully from the beginning, to write it [That which Luke knew], out for you in consecutive order, most excellent Theophilus***." Luke 1-3) The answer to the third question, "What is the book of Acts about" is fairly simple. The Book of Acts gives us an orderly account of the beginning of the church. In the first chapter of Acts, we discover the apostles standing by in Jerusalem, waiting for the promised Holy Spirit, which they eventually received in chapter two of Acts on the Day of Pentecost. The remaining 22 chapters of Acts reveal the results of the Holy Spirit in the lives of the disciples. The first 8 chapters of Acts are primarily about the ministry of Peter with a brief appearance by Saul at the end of chapter 7 and the beginning of chapter eight. The last 16 chapters of Acts are all about the conversion and ministry of Saul, who became the Apostle Paul.

Those who made up the inner circle of Jesus during His earthly ministry had an entirely different relationship with Him than Paul did. The disciples also took a very different path toward faith than Paul. Becoming a part of the ministry team was twofold for Saul. First, Saul had to become Paul; second, Paul had to convince the other Christians, most importantly the other apostles, that he was no longer in the business of murdering Christians.

Returning to the analogy of a person climbing a mountain to discover buried treasure, Paul's climb up the mountain was steeper than the climb of the other apostles because he had so much ground to make up. Paul, by the inspiration and instruction of the Holy Spirit, had to develop a relationship with Jesus, and then He had to develop relationships with the other believers. This process gave Paul a unique Christian maturation period, a unique perspective, and a unique relationship with his Lord and Savior. It also gave Paul a powerful testimony that none of the others had.

Paul's first encounter with the risen Lord occurred on the road to Damascus. (Acts 9:1-6). Saul had gone to the high priests seeking their permission to continue persecuting those belonging to The Way. On his way to Damascus, Saul encountered Jesus as a brilliant light that blinded him and caused him to fall to his knees. Throughout his entire life, Saul had been accustomed to seeing God through the prism of the Mosaic law and the traditions of his fathers. The very idea that a man could interact with, let alone have a relationship with the living God is exactly the kind of heresy that fueled Saul's passion to eradicate followers of this dead and buried rabbi from Nazareth named Jesus. Being addressed directly, personally, and undeniably by Jesus had to be equal parts convicting and overwhelming for Saul.

Scripture tells us that as Saul approached Damascus, a light from heaven suddenly flashed around him. Put another way, as Saul was traveling, he became surrounded on all sides, above, and below, with a brilliant and blinding light. We have all seen lightning from a distance and marveled. Some people have even been struck by lightning. Saul was surrounded, completely engulfed by light. In that instant, his environment was transformed into all-encompassing, incomprehensible light from heaven. Saul was instantly blinded, and he fell to his knees. At that moment, Saul heard a voice saying, "***Saul, Saul, why are you persecuting Me?***" (Acts 9:4). That which the original 12 disciples grew to understand about the deity of Jesus over a period of 3 and a half years became immediately apparent to Saul within seconds.

Saul was on a mission, and he had determined his own destination, but Jesus interrupted Saul's mission and gave him a new one. The same can be said for all disciples of Jesus, both then and now. Anyone who has come to Jesus has a Damascus Road experience of some sort. John, Andrew, Phillip, Simon, and all the rest were on their way to one place, and Jesus arrested their movement and put them on a different path. With Saul, however, he was so diametrically opposed to Jesus that his conversion demands close examination if we really want to know what Saul must have experienced in his relationship with Jesus. Whereas all the other disciples, even those who became apostles, were looking for the Messiah when they encountered Jesus, Saul was looking to prove that Jesus was not the Messiah. Although James and Jude, the brothers of Jesus, were probably skeptics most of if not all of Jesus' life, Saul was not just a skeptic; he was convinced that anyone who followed Jesus was guilty of heresy and deserving of death.

Once Saul was humbled, kneeling in the sand, blinded by the light from heaven, Jesus told Saul what to do, and thus began his relationship with the Lord. In that moment, Saul the pessimistic persecutor of Christ became Paul the prodigious prognosticator of Christianity. Paul's development took time; in fact, it took years for his public ministry to begin. During his maturation, when he worked with Barnabas and formed relationships with the other apostles, most notably Peter, Paul strengthened his relationship with Jesus through constant prayer. Paul did not have the benefit of being with Jesus in person to develop his relationship with the Lord, but the impact of spending time with Jesus was in no way diminished, and there was no other way for Paul to explain his encounter on the road to Damascus than as an encounter with the Living God.

Chapter Three

Jesus As Son Of God

In this chapter, we will examine scriptures that reveal what Jesus said or did, which distinguished Him as the Son of God. We will explore the ways Jesus submitted Himself to the will of God the Father and how He displayed this submission for others to see. We will also look at the prophetic scriptures His followers saw fulfilled in Him.

Being An Uncle Tom

In 1954, Thurgood Marshall argued the landmark case of Brown v. Board of Education before the United States Supreme Court. Marshall won the case, and the ruling overturned the 1896 Plessy v. Ferguson ruling, which granted federal legal standing to Jim Crow laws. The Plessy ruling allowed lawmakers to interpret the 14th Amendment as supporting the legality of public accommodations that were presumably separate but equal. During the Jim Crow era, public accommodations were indeed separate, but they were never equal. In effect, Plessy v. Ferguson gave legal authority for states to practice segregation, while Brown v. Board of Education used the 14th Amendment to end segregation in all states and made anti-segregation laws enforceable by the Federal Government.

I was born in Minneapolis, Minnesota, within a few years of the Brown v. Board of Education decision, and by the time I started school in the 1960's, integration in Minneapolis public schools was in full swing. I grew up during the period often referred to as "The turbulent 60's". My worldview was informed by the civil rights movement and fueled by lessons I was taught at home by my mother about slavery, emancipation, Jim Crow, the Civil Rights Movement, and my responsibility to fight/resist oppression.

Within this crucible of maturation, I learned that as a Black person, the last thing I wanted to be identified as was an Uncle Tom, which me and my peers believed was a Black person who had forsaken his Black heritage in order to cozy up to Whites. As a child growing up in the 60s, anytime we saw a Black person becoming too friendly with Whites, we would call them an Uncle Tom, and that was one of the worst insults one could issue. I didn't know it at the time, but the term "Uncle Tom" was derived from the 1852 novel by Harriet Beecher Stowe.

Having used this stinging insult often during my childhood, I did not actually read Stowe's novel until I was over 50 years old. I picked up a copy of the novel one summer and began to read it. By then, I was a Christian, and I realized within the first few chapters that I had completely misunderstood and therefore misjudged Stowe's main character. True, Uncle Tom was an enslaved Black man who was preoccupied with pleasing his master, but that was not due to some hatred, disdain, or even indifference toward other Blacks. Uncle Tom possessed a strong, deep, abiding love for enslaved Blacks, but he was also a Christian, legally bound to his earthly master. More than that, Uncle Tom was spiritually bound to His heavenly Master, and his behavior was motivated and guided by his faith.

As I read Stowe's novel, I was struck by how Uncle Tom was repeatedly dispatched on various errands by his first owner, Master Shelby, and wherever he went, all he needed to do was to invoke the name of his master to receive whatever he was sent for. Therefore, whatever Uncle Tom asked for in

Shelby's name was given to him, but he could not make a request in his own name or on his own authority.

I recall that during my childhood, my mother, a single parent, worked hard to make sure that her 8 children were respectful, responsible, and always obeyed the law. We lived in a community where relationships with others, even with the White merchants, were crucial. As such, my mother would often send me and one or two of my siblings to the local bakery, meat market, or pharmacy to pick up whatever was needed. In those circumstances, she would write down what was needed in a note and send us off to do the shopping. When we arrived at the merchant to whom we had been sent, we would present the note from my mother, and the baker, butcher, or pharmacist would give us the items on the list and then add the cost to the account my mother had established with them. If, however, I went to the baker on my own and requested a sack of cookies or donuts without the note from my mother, my request would be denied. In other words, whatever I asked for in my mother's name would be granted to me, but that which I requested in my own name was denied.

Jesus was appointed by God the Father as heir of all things. (Hebrews 1:2) Being heir includes rights, responsibility, and authority. In His capacity as Heir of all things, Jesus made a remarkable yet far too often misunderstood and misapplied statement. Jesus said, "***Whatever you ask in My name, that I will do, so that the Father may be glorified in the Son. If you ask Me anything in My name, I will do it.***" In the next verse, Jesus continues by saying, "***If you love Me, you will keep My commandments***." (John 14:13-15)

Like Uncle Tom, who made requests on behalf of his master, and like my siblings making requests on behalf of our mother, as Christians, we need to understand that when we are acting upon the will and the authority of the Heir, we can ask anything of Him in pursuit of His will, and it will be given. I say this scripture is misunderstood and misapplied because too many have taken it to mean that whatever they ask for, in pursuit of their own agenda, should be given, but that is not what Jesus is saying. Twice in these verses, Jesus emphasizes that the request must be made in ***His*** name, and He follows up by saying that if we love Him, we will keep ***His*** commandments.

The ministry of Jesus was and is missional. From the beginning, Jesus was drawing people to Himself to carry out His Father's mission. When Jesus's followers heard Him say that anything they ask in His name He will do, they would have understood this to mean that as they carry out their mission on behalf of Jesus, He would provide everything they need to be successful in doing His will. It is clear that this passage is about Jesus exercising His authority, for His purpose, to accomplish the will of His Father. Although we might be confused by what Jesus was saying here, His disciples never took His words as a blank check to have their own personal needs met and their own personal desires fulfilled. They were in effect Uncle Toms, and in the same sense, we ought to be Uncle Toms as well.

The Offensive Gospel

Jesus is, was, and always will be the most offensive and polarizing figure in human history. In February 2012, I watched the funeral coverage of Whitney Houston, who was adored by millions around the world for her incredible vocal talent and as an actress. Throughout the funeral coverage, people continued to state that Whitney was heaven-bound. When we look at social media, we see where people post pictures of someone who has died with the caption, RIP (Rest in Power) or (Rest in Peace). We have this notion that if a person is beloved, famous, popular, or just kind, there is a place reserved in heaven for them. I don't know whether or not Whitney Houston is in heaven, but God knows, and He has His criteria for who gets in and who does not. In a world where people demand tolerance and inclusiveness and want to believe that all roads lead to God, Jesus's words come off as intolerant, exclusive, and offensive.

Jesus gathered with His disciples for a final meal and, using His own garments as a towel, He washed and dried their feet, including those of Judas, whom He knew would betray Him. (John 13:5-12) As He washed the feet of His disciples, Jesus understood that God the Father had given all things into His hands and that He was Heir of all things. Jesus's time had come, and he was also aware that He would soon be returning to his Father. Peter initially refused to let Jesus wash his feet, but he gave in when Jesus explained the significance of what He was doing. After His interactions with Peter and after explaining the importance of love and humility to His disciples, Jesus said that one of them would betray Him.

Jesus dipped a morsel of bread, handed it to Judas, and said to him, "***What you do, do quickly***." (John 13:27) Once Judas left, Jesus began to explain that He would soon be leaving them, and His disciples did not understand why He was leaving or where He was going. It was Thomas who said to Jesus, "***Lord, we do not know where you are going. How do we know the way***?" (John 14:5). The response Jesus gave to Thomas in answer to this question laid out the path to heaven for all humanity in simple, unambiguous terms which left no room for an inclusive, ecumenical, theology. Jesus said, "***I***

am the way, the truth, and the life. No one comes to the Father but through Me." (John 14:6)

This simple statement of Jesus forms the basis for offense because, rather than affirming every other religion in an effort to find peace and common ground, with this statement, Jesus declared all other religions false. This places us as Christian Americans in a position wherein we must also be as offensive as Jesus. As Americans, we can affirm and even defend the rights guaranteed to all Americans under the 1st Amendment to the US Constitution, which protects the right to worship as we choose. However, as Christians, we affirm without apology that the ***only*** way to heaven is through Jesus. We can affirm a person's right to choose while remaining true to the fact that any choice other than Jesus will not lead to heaven.

This doctrine of truth is more offensive now than it was in the 1st century because, in the 21st Century, there are many more false religions, cults, and philosophies that did not exist then. In addition to this, the means of proliferating these false religions allows everyone greater ability to go their own way and forsake the truth of Christianity. Because true Christianity does not bow down to any false religion and it does not make accommodation for or presume equality with these false religions, true unadulterated Christianity becomes the most offensive religion because of its claims of exclusivity spoken by our Lord and Savior in John 14:6.

The statement Jesus made in John 14:6 was made to His disciples and not to the religious authorities. With this statement to His disciples Jesus set aside any notion of multiple paths to salvation, He declared with this statement that the only way to heaven was through Him. While this statement was/is offensive to people then and now who want an easier path which allows them to live life on their own terms, to His disciples, the statement was another powerful declaration of Jesus as the Son of God.

Jesus was speaking as One with authority, as the Heir of all things, and this would not have been missed by His disciples. Jesus spoke the words of John 14:6 during the final days of His earthly ministry, and by this time the disciples had been with Him for nearly three and one-half years. Hearing Jesus declare that He is the only way to the Father must have created an even deeper desire on the part of His disciples to spend as much time with Jesus as they possibly could before His departure to be with His Father.

Self-Incrimination

There is a very familiar provision within the Fifth Amendment to the US Constitution, which has been interpreted by the US Supreme Court to provide protection against self-incrimination. We all understand this to mean that we cannot be compelled to give statements in a court of law that we believe could cause us to incriminate ourselves. Simply put, we cannot be forced to testify against ourselves in a court of law. The section of the Fifth Amendment we are so familiar with says, "Nor shall any person be compelled in any criminal case to be a *witness against himself*." It is this provision that allows a person to "*Take the fifth*" in court and remain silent during their own trial or when they are being questioned for a crime.

The question often asked from Christian pulpits and even placed on bumper stickers is, "*If you were accused of being a Christian, would there be enough evidence to convict you*?" Since the first time I saw this question on a bumper sticker, I have regularly asked this question of myself. Does my life produce sufficient evidence to convict me if I were accused of being a Christian? I certainly hope so.

Judas had betrayed Jesus, and while Jesus prayed in the Garden of Gethsemane, Judas led a crowd of men carrying clubs to arrest Him. Having taken Him into custody, the men brought Jesus to the home of the High Priest and there they began to interrogate Him. Jesus was led to the council chambers of the Sanhedrin where they said to Him, "***If you are the Christ, [The Messiah prophesied in Old Testament Scripture] tell is.***" (Luke 23:66-71) Let's pay close attention to the response Jesus gave them. They asked if He was the Christ, but Jesus did not answer their question. Instead, He said, "***If I tell you, you will not believe; and if I ask a question, you will not answer.***" Then Jesus maneuvered their subsequent questions so that they actually identified Him as the Son of God. Jesus said, "***But from now on the Son of Man will be seated at the right hand of the power of God***". After He said this, they asked the crucial question, which led to Jesus's conviction. As Jesus stared down the court of His day, the question they asked Him was, "***Are you the Son of God, then?***" Jesus' answer was unambiguous, "***Yes, I am.***"

Jesus was facing a charge of blasphemy, and by answering as He did, Jesus claimed to be the Son of God, and thereby equal to God, possessing all the divine attributes of God. When Jesus said, ***Yes, I am***" He admitted that He was guilty as charged. Without any constitutional protection, let alone a fifth amendment provision, Jesus, knowing the consequences of self-incrimination did not waver for so much as a second. Of course, we understand that Jesus was not an American and He did not have a right not to self-incriminate. My point is that Jesus was happy to incriminate

Himself once they asked the right question, "***Are you the Son of God?***"

I said Jesus maneuvered the questioning and now I need to explain what I meant by this statement. The men said to Jesus, " If you are the Christ, tell us. I believe when it came to self-incrimination, Jesus wanted to go big. He knew He would be crucified, and He wanted to achieve maximum effect with His admission. Their initial remark was, "***If you are the Messiah, tell us***." If Jesus had simply responded by saying yes, He would have allowed them to define His identity, purpose, and ministry in their own terms. Jesus wanted them to reason for themselves who He really is using the very scriptures they studied regularly. This is not dissimilar to what Jesus did in John 8:58, when He used the Old Testament scripture, Exodus 3:14 and said to them, "***Before Abraham was born, I AM***." This brought them to the inescapable conclusion that Jesus was claiming to be God.

In this situation, Jesus took them back to another Old Testament scripture they were well familiar with. "***I kept looking in the night visions, and behold, with the clouds of heaven One like the Son of Man was coming, and He came up to the Ancient of Days [God the Father] and was presented before Him, and to Him was given dominion, glory, and a kingdom that all the peoples, nations, and men of every language might serve Him. His dominion is an everlasting dominion which will not pass away, and His kingdom is one which will not be destroyed.***" Daniel 7:13.

Jesus most often referred to Himself as the son of man in the New Testament, which is commonly believed to be a reference to His humanity. The term means that He was born of a human being and therefore, He was human. The reference Daniel made to “Son of Man” can be taken as a possessive reference, meaning that the person spoken of in Daniel’s prophecy was a gift ***to*** man as opposed to the first-century Aramaic colloquialism commonly understood as one who came ***from*** man. Having maneuvered the conversation in this way, Jesus distinguished Himself from other charismatic rabbis of the time who claimed to be some version of the prophesied messiah.

By using their own understanding of scripture, Jesus claimed the higher ground of being the One who fulfilled all prophesies and was presented before the Ancient of Days and given dominion [Heir] over all things. Jesus, facing these accusations with courage and conviction, laid the groundwork for the ministry of the apostles as they sought from that moment on to be more like their Lord. I believe that this is one of the lasting effects Jesus had on those who heard His admission.

Food For Thought

As we transport ourselves back 2,000 years and immerse ourselves in the lives of those who spent time with Jesus during His earthly ministry, there are times when, if we truly place ourselves into the cultural context of what we read, it becomes clear why the things He said and did were so dramatic, offensive, polarizing, and, of course, endearing. One of the many reasons I have such a high view of scripture is because I firmly believe that the words of the Bible are, by themselves, so shockingly transformative that, absent any human editorializing or pontification, they are radically sufficient to change lives. I believe that when preachers allow the scriptures to speak for themselves, the consciousness of those who are listening is shocked, and people are drawn to Jesus.

While many people may want to join hands and sing "*let there be peace on earth*," how can anyone not be shocked by the words of Jesus as He says things like, "***Do not think that I came to bring peace on earth? I did not come to bring peace but a sword. I came to set a man against his father, and a daughter against her mother, and a daughter-in-law against her mother-in-law.***" (Matthew 10:34) If being a Christian means being Christ-like, then rather than making people feel comfortable, we ought to be doing as Jesus did and making people feel the counter-cultural weight of scripture as it presses against the comfort of maintaining the status quo.

This is not to say that Jesus did not offer comfort; it is to say that He did not offer comfort as the world does. This is not to say that Jesus is not endearing; it is to say that Jesus is endearing only through the lens of God's Word, and He is offensive through the lens of human philosophy. As I study the interactions between Jesus and those who flocked to hear Him, and see the miracles He performed, I find one of His most powerful teachings is in His description of Himself as the bread of life. The way Jesus orchestrated this particular moment and then seized that moment to teach possibly one of His most important lessons is incredible.

In chapter six of John's gospel, we read about the feeding of the five thousand, followed by Jesus' walking on water. After Jesus got into the boat, the boat was immediately transported to the other side where they were going. The following day, the crowd of people who had been miraculously fed by Jesus the day before arrived looking for another show and probably hoping to receive another free meal in the process. With their minds fixed on dinner and a show, Jesus offered a message with eternal consequences.

When the crowds found Jesus on the other side of the lake, some of them opened the conversation by asking Him, "***Rabbi, when did you get here?***" Jesus did not beat around the bush; He got right to the heart of the matter by saying, "***Truly, truly, I say to you, you seek Me, not because you saw signs, but because you ate of the loaves and were filled.***" In other words, Jesus was saying they came to get more food. Jesus gave them a gentle reminder that they ought to be seeking the will of God, to which they responded by asking what they needed to do the works of God.

Jesus never missed an opportunity to speak to the people from the scriptures, and when they mentioned the manna provided by Moses, Jesus turned the tables and explained that it was not Moses but God the Father who provides true bread from heaven. Jesus went on to explain that spiritually speaking, they needed to ingest Him in order to experience eternal life as opposed to temporal life that comes through eating common bread. (John 6:26-35)

The profundity of what Jesus said here is so foundational to our faith, and He alluded to this principle earlier when He quoted Deuteronomy 8:3 to the devil, saying, "***It is written, man shall not live on bread alone, but on every word that proceeds out of the mouth of God.*** (Matthew 4:12) The point Jesus was making is that we must be filled up with Him, His character, His zeal for righteousness, His devotion to the Father, His life, in order to experience eternal life for ourselves. For anyone listening and actually paying attention, this moment would have been a game-changer. This is why I believe this would have been one of the most endearing moments of being in the presence of Jesus. In that moment, Jesus answered the quintessential question of humanity: how do I live fully while I am here on earth, and how do I experience life beyond the grave?

Believing Is Seeing

"***Now faith is the substance of things hoped for, the evidence of things not seen.***" (Hebrews 11:1) When my children were babies, I could take them anywhere, and they never asked where we were going. As they got older and understood that some destinations were preferable to others, whenever I said it's time to go, they would ask me where we were going. If I failed to answer their questions sufficiently, once we got into the car, the inquisition would only intensify. I didn't think about it at the time, but there is something unnerving about being in a vehicle and not knowing where you will end up. It's a little bit like a movie scene where someone has a bag placed over their head before being shoved into a van with no windows. Of course, while my children might have been frustrated with me for not promptly letting them know where we were going, I was hoping they would simply trust that our destination was necessary and that I meant nothing but good for them. Although my children loved me, I am not God, and there was no reason for them to trust me as God expects us to trust Him. As human beings, even with the best of intentions, we should never expect another human being to trust us as completely as we are expected to trust God.

The word our Bibles translate as faith is the Greek word *pistis* and it is used 248 times in the New Testament. The word *pistis*, which can also be translated as hope, trust, or believe, is used 99 times in John's gospel alone, and the word is most often used in the New Testament in its verb form. The practical implication is that for everything we have faith in, hope for, trust or believe in, there ought to be a corresponding action.

If my children had faith in me, the corresponding action would have been to get in the car without question. If one trusts in something, they cease worrying about the same. If one has faith in the strength of a rope, they will put their full weight on the rope and repel down a cliff. If one believes in the lethal capacity of a handgun, they will move out of the way when someone points a gun in their direction. According to Hebrews 11:6, it is impossible to please God without having faith in Him, and the ministry of Jesus is about presenting God the Father in clear and compelling terms to transition us from faith in the law, human institutions, and ourselves, to faith in the unfailing power of God.

A person who has put their faith in Jesus is not converted through facts or evidence, and a non-believer does not remain unconverted for lack of facts or evidence. An unbeliever is converted because they know they are perishing without Jesus, and they place a higher value on Him than they place on their sin. A non-believer to whom Christ has revealed Himself remains unconverted because their sin has greater value to them than their salvation.

Jesus stood before a large crowd and prayed to the Father asking Him to glorify His name. In response God the Father said in a voice that could be heard by them all, "***I have both glorified it, and will glorify it again.***" (John 12:28) Hearing this, the crowd said it must have been thunder or perhaps an angel. Jesus explained that the voice came so that they could hear and believe. Jesus explained that judgement was at hand, because knowing the truth, they would now be held accountable to that truth. This is an incredible example of hard-heartedness, wherein people can hear the truth and refuse to believe it.

Even after seeing all the miracles Jesus did and hearing the things he taught, which came right out of the scriptures they knew all too well, they refused to believe. Jesus quoted Isaiah who had predicted that people could not believe because their eyes would be blinded, and their hearts would be hardened. Jesus then gave the crowd a stark warning and said, "***If anyone hears My sayings and does not keep them, I do not judge him; for I did not come to judge the world, but to save the world. He who rejects Me and does not receive my sayings, has one who judges him; the word I spoke is what will judge him at the last day.***" (John 12 47-48)

Over the course of several months, I shared my faith with an old friend, and I thought if I just presented the right argument, or better yet, if I just read the right scripture, she would believe. I was absolutely wrong about this, and at one point I looked at her while she stood steadfast, refusing to believe, and I realized how far beyond me her salvation was. As Christians, our mission is to share the truth, not to convince anyone of the truth. I had a seminary professor who put this phenomenon so very well when he said, it's sometimes more effective to talk to God about people then to talk to people about God.

I explained to my unbelieving friend that there was nothing I could say that would convince her the Bible is true, that God is real, and that He loves her. Like the crowds that Jesus faced, people see the miracles in their own lives, they see the complexity of creation, and they witness the grace of God, yet they will make every excuse under the sun to dismiss the truth. It comes down to the simple yet profound truth that seeing is not believing, believing is seeing.

Audacious Arrogance Towards The Heir

When I was a teenager my best friend's father owned a business, and he employed several men to work for him. My friend's father also hired the two of us to work at the business. He paid us a fair wage, and he had reasonable expectations of us. Over the years I became very attached to my friend's father, and I believe he treated me with genuine affection. However, I was not the owner of that business, and I was not the heir, my friend was the heir. My friend never lorded this over me and he never treated me as an underling. However, despite the grace afforded me through my relationship with the father and his son, if I had tried to usurp the rightful position of my friend within the company in an attempt to establish my own dominion, it would have been an unpardonable act of audacious arrogance. My rightful place within that company was one of humility and gratitude; the same is true for us as followers of Jesus in the church.

In Mark 12:1-12, speaking to members of the Sanhedrin, Jesus told the parable of the vine-growers. Knowing that Jesus was speaking to the religious authorities helps us understand this parable, and as always, context is crucial to understanding. The religious authorities were defending what they believed to be their own established domain. They had set themselves up as pious leaders of God's people and claimed to be the righteous ones who held the keys to godliness. The parable of the vine-growers was the means Jesus used to inform these men that they had wrongfully taken something which never belonged to them. With this in mind, we can see that the man in this parable who planted the vineyard is God the Father, the vine-growers are any human authority that tries to establish spiritual dominion over the people of God, and Jesus is the son, sent to redeem that which is the rightful property of His Father.

Since Moses came down from Mount Sinai with the ten commandments, people have been seduced by the temptation to position themselves as a lightning rod for God's word, disbursing the wisdom of God from within themselves. True Christian leaders hold fast to the mindset of John the Baptist who said, "***He must increase, but I must decrease***." (John 3:30) These words of John were not a new or novel idea, they have always been the Christian mandate, and for those with knowledge of the scriptures, for those who are gifted orators, and those who are skilled, charismatic leaders, this is the ongoing battle; to lead God's people, accepting none of His glory, and deferring all accolades to Jesus. The words of the parable were boldly proclaimed by Jesus to remind these religious authorities that He is the only true authority and the only true heir. In this situation the reaction was split between the religious authorities who were offended, and the seekers of truth who were awestruck.

Sometimes arrogance is born out of complacency. The Pharisees had become accustomed to treating the people of God and the religion of God as if it were their own, and the parable was Jesus's way of shaking them out of their complacency. It may be difficult to imagine the shocking effect this parable would have had on those who heard Jesus speak but it helps to keep in mind that standing up to the religious authorities of this time had severe consequences and this encounter between Jesus and the Sanhedrin was one of many that eventually led to His crucifixion. Jews simply did not engage in debate with these men for fear that they would at the very least be ostracized and put out of the synagogues or barred from temple worship, which was the epicenter of Jewish life. Jesus stood up to bullies then as we should stand up to bullies now. Those gathered to hear this interaction understood that the parable was a direct challenge to the arrogant audacity of the established religious authority of that day.

When Grown Folks Talk

Someone, possibly Mark Twain once wrote that it is better to remain silent and risk being thought of as a fool, than to speak and remove all doubt. When I was a child one of my favorite memories was watching my parents and other elders discussing grown up stuff. As a child, I was not invited in on these conversations, and no one asked my opinion. As I grew into adulthood those same people would sometimes invite me into the conversations, but I was only able to weigh in by invitation. This may seem odd and even unfair by today's standards, but I learned some important lessons by sitting, listening, and holding my place. I learned to avail myself of the wisdom of my elders, and I learned how to hold my tongue until I had something of value to offer.

On two separate occasions, Jesus took Peter, John, and James with him as he went off to pray, and I want to look at both instances separately. The first time He did this was relatively early in His ministry and it is believed that they went to Mount Tabor; the second time they went to the garden of Gethsemane. In both situations Jesus instructed His disciples to remain behind and to pray, and in both situations, the disciples fell asleep. I find it difficult to criticize these men for not learning after the first instance of sleeping on the job because I can tend to be very hardheaded and slow to pick up on things myself. Rather than being critical of these beloved disciples, I want us to pick up on the lessons we can learn from their experiences and better understand how these experiences impacted their relationship with Jesus and their future ministries.

Eight days prior to Jesus going up on the mountain to pray and directly after He fed the 5,000, Jesus taught His disciples that He would suffer and be rejected by the elders, chief priests, and the scribes. Jesus taught them the meaning of sacrificial living, and He asked the disciples who they thought He was. It was Peter who answered the question correctly saying, "***The Christ, the Son of God***." (Luke 9:18-27). As Jesus went up on the mountain, He prayed and was transfigured. It was there on the mountain that Jesus met with Elijah and Moses. During the discussion with His disciples where Jesus asked who people thought He was, one of the responses was, that people thought He was Elijah. As Jesus was transfigured, he carried on a conversation with Elijah and the brilliant scene as well as the vibrant conversation between Jesus, Elijah, and Moses awoke His disciples from their slumber.

I think if we are honest, most of us can identify with Peter more than the rest of the disciples. Peter is the one who would get it right in one interaction with Jesus and then stick his foot in his mouth the next moment. I began this section with reference to being a child in a room where adults were carrying on conversations. My role in these conversations was to listen and learn. Peter, having risen from his slumber, should have listened silently like a child and learned.

Rather than remaining silent, Peter stuck his foot in his mouth and spoke. In response, God the Father addressed Peter directly saying, "***This is My Son, My Chosen One; listen to Him!***" (Luke 9:35). Paraphrase, Peter, shut up and listen, you might learn something. Hearing the voice of God declaring Jesus as His Son, must have been the clearest affirmation of Jesus' claim to be the Son of God. In Peter's defense, it was probably two or three years until the next time Jesus instructed His disciples to watch His back and pray, but this time had to have made a profound impression on Peter, James, and John.

The Flanking Maneuver

As you read about the epic battles in the Old Testament you cannot miss the reoccurring flanking maneuvers used by Israel to decimate opposing armies. Flanking maneuvers were also used by opposing armies against Israel. The concept was simple but brilliant. As the opposing army prepared for a frontal assault, the general would dispatch a segment of the army to circle around and attack from behind, exploiting the exposed flanks of the enemy. The maneuver was used so often one wonders why armies did not anticipate the move. When it comes to spiritual warfare Jesus is the master strategist, and knowing that He would soon be departing, in this second example of Jesus instructing the disciples to watch and pray. Jesus was teaching His disciples a valuable lesson about protecting their exposed flanks.

Jesus understands that prayer is our most potent weapon in spiritual warfare and as He entered His most vulnerable circumstance, He prepared to pray perhaps His most consequential prayer. Jesus sent the three disciples. Peter, James, and John, to take up positions behind Him and to cover Him in prayer. Jesus returned three times to find them fast asleep. (Mark 14:32-42 Luke 22:39-46) The disciples were not men of war, they were fishermen, and Jesus did not need their prayers for His protection, they needed to learn the strategic value and importance of prayer for times yet to come when they would be most vulnerable. Whenever we face consequential moments in our lives, when the stakes are high, when the enemy stands to make significant gains, that is the time for our most fervent prayers, and it is no time to slumber. When I look back on seasons of my life when the enemy gained a foothold, I can see where I failed to cover my flanks with my own prayers or to solicit the prayers of my friends and family.

Upon entering the garden of Gethsemane Jesus said, "***My soul is deeply grieved to the point of death, remain here and keep watch***." (Mark 14:34) When Jesus returned, He found His disciples sleeping and he said, "***Simon, are you asleep? Could you not keep watch for one hour***?" (Mark 14:37) Flanking maneuvers are all about exploiting points of vulnerability in the enemy's defenses, and there are three crucial points of vulnerability revealed by Jesus in these verses:

The vulnerability of grief. Jesus stated that He was "Deeply Grieved". Jesus made this declaration to His disciples, and it was not the way they were accustomed to seeing Him. When Jesus was confronted by angry mobs that wanted to kill Him, He remained unmoved, He simply did what needed to be done and said what needed to be said. When Jesus was faced with thousands of hungry followers, there was no indication that the situation challenged Him in the least, He simply broke the bread He had, gave thanks, and distributed it to the hungry masses. When the wine ran out at the wedding in Cana, Jesus calmly sent the servants to fill up the empty jugs with water and then take them to the head waiter. When the storms threatened to tear the boat apart, Jesus kept sleeping and when He awoke, He simply rebuked the wind. Now, toward the end of His life, the disciples witnessed

Jesus in a state of deep grief that rocked Him to the core of His being. Jesus understood what He was about to face, and He understood the eternal consequences of the next 48 hours of His life; it was these facts that caused our Lord and Savior to be "Deeply Grieved". It was for this reason He called His friends to pray for Him and to keep watch, so that they could witness and participate in the transforming power of prayer.

The vulnerability of dependance. Jesus prayed, openly placing His circumstances into the hands of His Father. Those of us who have been Christians for a while have grown so familiar with the words of Jesus in the garden that they may not land on us with the gravity they deserve. Knowing what was to come and acknowledging the option for the cup to pass from Him, Jesus subordinated the will of His flesh to the divine will of His Father, and He trusted Him completely with the outcome. There is an important distinction between a person trusting Jesus for their salvation, and Jesus trusting God the Father in that moment. When we put our trust in Jesus, we are giving up a worthless existence so that we may gain a life of meaning and an eternity of joy. By contrast, Jesus came from eternal glory and joy in order experience the full measure of humanity only without sin. Put another way, we gave up nothing for everything, and Jesus gave up everything for the adversity of the human experience, and the most humiliating and painful death imaginable. This is the level of trust and vulnerability ensconced within Jesus's prayer in the garden of Gethsemane.

The vulnerability of temptation. Jesus instructed His disciples to "***Keep watch***" and when He found them sleeping, He said to them "***Keep watching and praying that you may not come into temptation.***" Jesus' flanks were exposed while He prayed, but His concern was that His disciples might come into temptation. A thorough study of the Bible from the Old Testament to the New Testament reveals our human predilection for pragmatism. However, the most powerful tool at our disposal in dire circumstances is prayer. Intercessory prayer which is what Jesus commissioned Peter and the other disciples to engage in is extremely powerful, but it can also be fraught with complications because the one praying is one degree removed from the immediate adversity of the moment. James, the brother of Jesus wrote, "***The effective prayer of a righteous man can accomplish much***." (James 5:16) One of my favorite examples of effective or fervent prayer is seen in the Book of Acts when Herod had Peter arrested and put in jail. As Peter lay asleep in jail the people of the church prayed fervently for him and an angel of the Lord came into the prison and released him. (Acts 12:1-11)

Effective or fervent prayer, especially intercessory prayer requires focus and persistence. It is interesting to me that Jesus took three of His disciples to Gethsemane, but He singled out Peter for rebuke even though the scripture makes it clear that John, James, and Peter, were sleeping. My point is that Jesus seemed to reserve the majority of His rebukes for Peter, and it was Peter's life and ministry that required him, perhaps more than any of the other apostles except Paul, to develop a discipline of effective, focused, persistent, (Fervent), prayer. Jesus took the moment at Gethsemane to teach Peter a valuable lesson about prayerfully standing guard in moments of great adversity. Jesus was teaching Peter to develop the discipline of prayer and to expect powerful outcomes from prayer, despite being vulnerable to temptation, whether the temptation manifests in distraction, sin, or simply fatigue.

This prayerful, rather than pragmatic approach to facing challenging circumstances was as counter-intuitive then as it is now. In that moment, the disciples with Jesus saw firsthand how the Son of God trusted in His Father and the powerful result of doing so. It is difficult to imagine how anyone could witness what these disciples saw in that moment without being profoundly impacted.

Chapter Four

Leader

First century Jews were hungry for leadership; as a people, they were in a desperate situation, and they had waited centuries for the messiah that had been promised in scripture. Certainly, Jesus fulfilled all the prophesies written about the Messiah, but His leadership went far beyond the expectations laid out in the ancient scriptures. Jesus drew people to Himself like no other person could and in this chapter, we will walk alongside Jesus and discover the ways in which His followers experienced His leadership.

Biblical Lessons In leadership

I was once asked during an interview if I thought I was a good leader. I told the interviewer that effective leadership, while difficult to execute, is fairly simple; it's about having a vision and inspiring others to embrace and then follow that vision. The Bible has many incredible examples of leadership, both good and bad, we only need to read it with a desire to learn these leadership lessons and dig in. Book stores are jammed full of tomes on leadership. Men and women who have attained some level of success in business, government, or even ministry put their leadership concepts in writing, and those who aspire to greatness consume these publications almost faster than they can be written. But I believe the best examples of leadership are found in both the Old and New Testaments of the Bible.

Because our interest is in the leadership of Jesus, we will confine our focus to the New Testament, but for the sake of balance, I strongly recommend a study of 1st and 2nd Samuel, 1st and 2nd Kings, and 1st and 2 Chronicles. These books offer some of the best examples of what the Bible teaches about leadership. In those Old Testament scriptures, you will see how King David, by the grace of God built an enduring legacy using key leadership principals. I have written extensively about King David in my book, "Endeared – Pursuing the heart of God," and you may also find some valuable insights on leadership by reading it.

To begin our study of Jesus as a leader I want to draw our attention to an interesting similarity between something both King David and Jesus did. Both King David and Jesus assembled an effective team of followers who bought into their vision. After assembling an effective team, they taught and empowered those teams to carry their vision forward. For King David, this team was a group of vagabonds who were drawn to him during his flight from King Saul. For Jesus, it was a group of fishermen and others who would not have been anyone's first choice for building a leadership team. In both cases, the gifts and talents each team possessed were developed and honed to the point where they functioned with a sense of purpose and determination.

John Maxwell, one of the many people who have written extensively on leadership once wrote, "*He who thinks he leads, but has no followers, is only taking a walk.*" When we read the Bible, we observe that it is a leadership vacuum that creates both the need for a leader, and the pool of potential followers. In addition to articulating a compelling vision and a path forward, successful leaders need to assemble and then develop a strong team that will move the leader's vision forward.

Assembling The Team

All four of the gospels include the calling and formation of Jesus's core group of disciples who went on to become His

Apostles. The fact that this calling is featured in each of the four gospels indicates the significance of Jesus calling disciples. In a sense, understanding what occurred when Jesus called and assembled His team of twelve is essential to understanding how and why people were drawn to Jesus in the 1st century and why billions continue to be drawn to Him today. The gospel of John provides some important background and context for Jesus calling the twelve disciples which made up His inner circle, so we will begin with his gospel. The calling is not laid out sequentially from Matthew through John so in order to learn what took place before Jesus called the 12, we have to start with John and then work our way through the synoptic gospels.

Each of the four gospels offers a different perspective on many of the same events. In some ways it's like a police officer taking statements from several witnesses who were present when a crime or traffic accident occurred. In these situations, it is not uncommon for each person to offer a different version of the same incident based upon their individual perspective; all versions can be true without them all being the same. Therefore, it is vital that we read all four gospels if we want to see the full story. If we only read the account of Jesus gathering His disciples recorded in Matthew's gospel, it might appear as though Jesus was just strolling along the Galilean seashore when He randomly came across a bunch of fishermen He didn't know. (Matthew 4:12) However, with the background provided in John chapter 1, we can see that by the time Matthew's narrative picks up with gathering the twelve, Jesus had already met these men and had begun to build a relationship with them.

In Matthew 4:18 we read, "***Now as Jesus was walking by the Sea of Galilee, He saw two brothers, Simon who was***

called Peter, and Andrew his brother." By reading this verse in isolation we could get the impression that at this moment Jesus had not yet met Simon or his brother Andrew. However, when we read John 1:35-51 we learn that Jesus already had a relationship with these men because it was Jesus who gave Simon the name Peter during their initial encounter which occurred prior to John the Baptist being taken into custody. It was only after this initial introduction that Jesus went to Galilee. (John 1:43) Therefore, when we read in Matthew 4:12 that Jesus saw Andrew and Simon who was called Peter, it is evident that Jesus knew these brothers prior to this encounter. By studying Matthew and John we now understand that it was after His initial meeting with Andrew, Peter, Philip, and Nathanael, and after John the Baptist was taken into custody that Jesus walked along the Galilean seashore and called His disciples. This knowledge removes the randomness of their encounter on the seashore and offers a more thoughtful, strategic view of how Jesus called the disciples.

Theodore Roosevelt once said, "*People don't care how much you know until they know how much you care.*" Convinced that he had found the Messiah, Andrew brought Simon to Jesus, who began spending time with Andrew, Simon, Phillip, and Nathanael. John the Baptist introduced Andrew to Jesus, and it was after this initial introduction that Jesus met Simon, Philip, and Nathaneal. During this introduction John directed his disciples to follow Jesus, but they did not necessarily follow Jesus because John directed them to do so. The disciples followed Jesus after hearing His message and spending time with Him. Jesus invested time in these men, building relationships, sharing a vision, and inspiring them to believe that He is the promised Messiah.

As Jesus walked along the seashore, he found Peter and Andrew attending to the family fishing business. Having spent time with Jesus and being fully convinced that He is the Messiah, all the disciples needed was an invitation to follow, and Jesus gave it to them. In response, the two men dropped what they were doing and followed Jesus. With Andrew and Peter in tow, Jesus next came across James and his brother John casting their nets into the sea. James and John were partners with Andrew and Peter, and they also dropped their nets and followed. (Matthew 4:18-22) (Mark 1:14-20) (Luke 5:1-11) It is reasonable to conclude that James and John were influenced to follow Jesus because they saw Andrew and Peter following. This is not unlike the way we can pique the interest of our friends and family when they see us following Jesus.

After Jesus spoke with Simon and gave him the name Peter, Jesus went to Galilee and found Phillip and Nathanael in the same city where Peter and Andrew lived. Jesus spoke directly to Philip and Nathanael in a way that made it clear He knew them, just as He demonstrated that He knew Simon. (John 1:43-51). Jesus gathered followers in the 1st century the same way He does now; Jesus sees directly into our lives, our pain, our vulnerability, and our struggles, just as He did with His initial disciples. While acknowledging that He knows and cares for us, Jesus replaces condemnation with purpose and acceptance. This is what the early disciples experienced in the presence of Jesus, and it is what we all feel when we come to Jesus today.

It is clear from scriptures the disciples were expecting a Messiah, and although John the Baptist had told them Jesus was that Messiah, they didn't follow Jesus simply because they were looking for a Messiah nor did they do so because

John told them Jesus was the Messiah; they followed Jesus because He demonstrated that He was the fulfillment of their expectations. This is how effective leaders build effective teams, they step into a vacuum, create relationships by demonstrating that they care, and then they lay out the vision for a path forward, toward a desired objective. Multitudes of people became disciples of Jesus, but it was a much smaller group that made up His inner-circle, and only 12 were identified by name as His original disciples.

Assembling Apostles

One of my favorite preachers made a shocking statement during a Sunday sermon by saying, "*We are all God's creation, but we are not all God's children*". Evangelist Billy Sunday once said that "*Going to church doesn't make you a Christian any more than going to a garage makes you an automobile*". I believe the point both of these men were making is that being a Christian is a choice. Being a Christian functions contrary to any western, politically correct, constructs of inclusivity. In fact, to be a Christian is to be part of an elite segment of humanity. The invitation to become a Christian is open to all, but not all of God's creation accepts the invitation to become one of His children.

My point in providing the above quotes is that there is a distinct difference between being a disciple and being an Apostle. I further state that having the title Apostle is not the same as behaving as an Apostle. Being a disciple simply means to be a student of Christianity, it means one has a curiosity to learn about the faith. Being an Apostle means to be sent out into the world to spread the good news of Jesus Christ. Anyone who accepts the call to become a Christian is then given the great commission to go and make disciples of all the nations. Jesus gave this great commission to His original 12 Apostles, and it has been a doctrine of our faith ever since. (Matthew 28:19) At this point, I want to take a look at who Jesus selected as the 12 Apostles, and how these twelve men might have experienced being called as a part of this elite team of 1st century believers.

As I have already noted, there are some parallels between the way King David assembled his team and the way Jesus assembled His team, and I find it very interesting how both men saw something in people others in society had discarded. While David was fleeing King Saul, he gathered a group of 400 men described as "***Everyone who was in distress, and everyone who was in debt, and everyone who was discontented gathered to him***." (1 Samuel 22:1-2) Several of the men who were drawn to David when he was on the run from King Saul were relatives of his, including his brothers and his nephews. For the most part these were men who would not have been respected within society, and they felt a connection between their own status as outcasts and that of David who had been ejected from King Saul's court. These were men who witnessed David's leadership abilities during the time he was a commander in Saul's army.

Jesus also gathered an unlikely group of people to make up His inner circle. Like David's band of warriors, Jesus's disciples included men such as Matthew the tax collector, a man who not only was odious to his fellow Jews, he was despised by them. Matthew's calling is significant in that it is mentioned in the gospels of Mark, Luke, and Matthew. Therefore, it seems wise to look deeper into the significance of Jesus calling Matthew as part of His team, and what the gospel writers had to say about it.

Collecting The Tax Collector

In his song, "*Take me to the alley,*" *released in 2016, Gregory Porter elucidates a core tenet of Jesus's message,* which is that He came to save the lost, not the lofty. Porter's song speculates that if Jesus were to return right now, rather than being attracted to those who use their material wealth to demonstrate fealty to Jesus, He would be drawn to the downtrodden and those on the fringes of society who are in need of salvation. In the gospels, we are presented with a Jesus who is unmoved by a person's station in life and more drawn to people who are willing to give up material wealth in pursuit of a higher calling.

As Jesus assembled His motley crew of disciples, he rounded out the team by calling a man no one would have wanted to associate with. Tax collectors were Jews who did the bidding of the Roman government by collecting taxes from their fellow Jews. In the process, they often collected more than was due and held on to the excess funds for themselves. Tax collectors made their living from the oppression of other Jews, and for this reason, they were hated.

There was no shortage of tax collectors to be found, but Jesus set His eyes on Matthew, also called Levi. In the gospel of Matthew, we read that Jesus saw a man called Matthew, sitting in the tax collector's booth, and He said to him, " Follow me. (Matthew 9:9). In Mark's gospel, we read that as Jesus walked along the seashore, He saw Levi, the son of Alphaeus, sitting in the tax booth, and He said to him, " Follow me. (Mark 2:13-14). However, Luke adds two additional pieces of information to the narrative.

The first new piece of information added by Luke is that after Jesus called Matthew, he "***Left everything behind, and got up and began to follow Him***" (Luke 5:27-28). Both Matthew and Mark tell us that after Jesus called Matthew, He ate with several tax collectors, but the second thing Luke tells us, which is not in the other gospels, is that it was Levi who gave the large reception for Jesus where He ate with the tax collectors. (Luke 5:29) While Jesus ate with the tax collectors, the Pharisees questioned why He and His disciples were eating with sinners, and this is where Jesus puts His ministry into focus by saying, "***It is not those who are well who need a physician, but those who are sick. I have not come to call the righteous but sinners to repentance***."

I want to make sure we see what the narratives in all the gospels tell us about Jesus calling Matthew as one of His disciples. When we read the Bible, to truly understand what is written, at times it is crucial that we suspend our 21st-century mindset, and reading about Matthew the tax collector's calling is one of those circumstances in which we must do so. Prior to Matthew's calling, we read about the fishermen, Andrew, Simon, James, and John, leaving their family fishing business and immediately following Jesus.

It is easy for us to grasp the fact that these men made their living on the water, fishing, and when they walked away from the family business, their fathers were left to carry on with only hired servants. We intuitively understand that these men were giving up their livelihood to pursue a call from the Messiah. However, to fully grasp what Matthew did we have to consider his actions from a 1st century Jewish point of view. As a tax collector Matthew's means of income required him to put himself at enmity with his fellow Jews. If things did not work out well with Jesus the fishermen could always go back to fishing, but Matthew left the wealth, comfort, and the protection of his position to follow Jesus. The risk to

Matthew was that if things did not work out with Jesus, he had already burned bridges with his fellow Jews. To further isolate himself, Matthew publicly embraced Jesus among his fellow tax collectors by throwing a banquet in His honor.

Jesus often did things to get under the skin of the religious authorities. For example, many of His miracles were performed on the Sabbath, which was in violation of the Jewish traditions, and these deeds were either reported to the religious authorities or witnessed by them. I believe this was intentional because by breaking their traditions, Jesus was afforded an opportunity to teach on important spiritual truths that contradicted and corrected those traditions. By calling a tax collector, eating with him, and inviting this tax collector to become part of His core team for proliferating the gospel, Jesus upended the bankrupt theology of the religious authorities and charted a new path toward ministering in the present and securing eternal salvation for us.

In a sense, the manner in which Jesus assembled His inner circle of men told a story. This story was woven into the details of Jesus calling the twelve, and with it, He readjusts our perspectives on what success looks like, how to live for God, and how to honor Him. Matthew was the last of the 12 to be called, but in some ways, I think His calling was more significant than the previous 11; not because of who Matthew was or what He eventually accomplished as an evangelist, but because of what it represented for Jesus to call Matthew and to include him as a disciple.

Developing Disciples

Good or bad, right or wrong, wise or foolish, effective or feckless, leaders are almost always teachers. An effective leadership tool is to offer knowledge or wisdom to those seeking enlightenment, and leaders learn to step into the knowledge void and offer solutions that resonate with those hungry for a sense of purpose and direction. Disciples are people who submit themselves to the teaching and organizational infrastructure offered by a leader. In this section, we will look at the methods Jesus used to demonstrate that He has what His disciples are looking for and what they need. I am using the present tense here intentionally because Jesus uses the same method now that He used in the 1st century. Even evil and maniacal leaders find a way of stepping into a vacuum of knowledge and offering a solution, but in each case where evil people offer leadership solutions, their legacy never endures. Jesus, by contrast, has built an enduring legacy of disciple-making that continues to this day.

John began his gospel by making the case for Jesus' deity, after which he went on to discuss the role of John the Baptist as forerunner for the ministry of Jesus. The Priests and Levites asked John if he was the Christ, Elijah, or the Prophet. John the Baptist said, "***I am a voice crying in the wilderness, make straight the way of the Lord.***" (John 1:19-23) This response by John was not a spontaneous utterance; it came from the Old Testament scriptures in Isaiah 40:3. By the time Jesus stepped onto the scene, John's pre-determined ministry was at its peak, and his mission was to prepare the way for the Messiah.

As a preacher with a compelling message of truth, John the Baptist had many disciples. One day, as John stood with two of his disciples, Jesus approached, and John said, "Behold, the Lamb of God!" (John 1:36). One of the two disciples with John that day was Andrew, the brother of Simon Peter. Andrew went with Jesus to where he was staying and spent time with Him. After spending time with Jesus, Andrew became convinced that he had found the Messiah spoken of in the Old Testament prophecies. Andrew returned to his brother Simon and said, "***We have found the Messiah***." (John 1:41) Andrew then brought Simon to Jesus who looked at him and said, "***You are Simon the son of John; you shall be called Cephas (Peter).***" (John 1:42). It is difficult to resist being drawn to someone who looks at you, sees you, knows you, and desires you to know him. That is the culmination of events that started with John fulfilling his ministry to baptize people, prepare the way of the Lord, and then direct his followers to follow Jesus.

Before we move forward, I want to review this chain of events:

- John the Baptist was born to proclaim the arrival of the promised Messiah, and he dedicated his life to that calling.
- John passed the torch and encouraged his disciples to follow Jesus
- Andrew spent time with Jesus and became convinced that he had found the Messiah
- Andrew found his brother Simon and told him that he had found the Messiah.
- Andrew then brought Simon to Jesus.
- Jesus looked at Simon and saw him.
- Jesus changed Simon's name to Peter.
- Peter followed Jesus.

Lowering The Bar

As I consider the aspects of Jesus's personality that are most endearing to me, I must confess that I love the way He showed complete disregard for the conventions and traditions of men. Jesus refused to bend or in any way modify His ministry to conform to the expectations of the masses. In fact, so much of what Jesus did appears to be His way of pointing out the impotence of common sense. We examined one example of this in the section, "Assembling the Apostles," where Jesus gathered the dregs of society to build His team of evangelists, which defied conventional wisdom. In this section, we will discuss the peculiar decision of Jesus to wash the feet of His disciples. Throughout time, from the 1st century, prior to the 1st century, and into this modern era, kings and other rulers have expected and often demanded to be served, but Jesus came not to be served, but to serve. (Matthew 20:28, Mark 10:45, John 13:1)

Recently, I had a conversation with a friend who is not a Christian, and I told her that God loves her. A few minutes later, she said, while shaking her head, God loves me even though I do not believe in Him. This was not a question; it was her way of pointing out the impossible inequity of God loving someone who does not love Him. In her mind, this makes no sense. As human beings, we are hard-wired with a transactional concept of love. We give to the extent that others give to us, we leverage advantages to better position ourselves, and when we have any amount of power or authority over others, it is our human nature to use that power to get others to meet our needs. Christianity and the message of the cross say, I love you even when you do not love me, and I love you more than you love me.

The story of Jesus washing the feet of His disciples is widely known by Christians and non-Christians alike, but I think this moment in the ministry of Jesus reveals a very profound truth in an extremely powerful and dramatic way, which rejects our natural human default to interact with one another pragmatically and transactionally. The gospel of John sets the scene for the last supper by telling us what was taking place before, during, and after the supper. In this description, John tells us that before the feast, Jesus knew His hour had come, that he was going to depart from this world, and that He would soon return to His father. (John 13:1) During the supper, the devil put it into the heart of Judas Iscariot to betray Jesus. (John 31:2) Also during the supper, Jesus, knowing that His Father had put all things into His hands, that He had come from God, and that He was returning to God, got up, set aside His garments, and prepared to wash the feet of His disciples.

Prior to the supper, the devil, knowing this was his last opportunity to strike a blow, made his play by putting it into the heart of Judas to betray Jesus. The devil's actions were pragmatic and based upon his presumption of a transactional response. The devil thought that if he moved to betray Jesus and have Him killed, Jesus would respond by developing a battle plan in response. However, the response of Jesus was to prepare His disciples to minister to one another with love and humility. This is what Jesus always does, he defies conventional wisdom and common sense by overcoming hatred and evil with humility and love.

I know churches sometimes practice foot washing ceremonies, but I cannot imagine anything in these ceremonies that might compare with washing the dirty, mangled, unkept feet of twelve first-century disciples who walked in sandals over rough, rocky terrain every day of their lives. The humility that Jesus displayed in this act of foot washing cannot be overstated. In the first century, when people gathered for a meal, they would wash their feet upon entering the home. In some circumstances, the wealthy might have a servant wash the feet of their guests. To wash one's own feet is not remarkable, but to wash the feet of someone else, one would need to get down on their knees and into a posture similar to that of submission. Therefore, it would go far beyond simple hospitality for a host to wash the feet of their guests. When Jesus removed His own garment, got down on His knees, and washed the feet of His students (Disciples), he demonstrated extreme humility. Jesus went further by using this foot washing to teach His disciples the nature of Christian ministry as one of service and humility rather than control and dominance.

The friend I mentioned previously could not comprehend a God who would love her when she does not believe in Him. The devil was not prepared for Jesus to face betrayal with forgiveness and humility. The foot washing was Jesus teaching His disciples how to respond to a world that continues to operate out of the devil's playbook. We only have Peter's reaction to the foot washing recorded in scripture, but the effect this act had on all the disciples, given this first century context, must have left an indelible imprint on their lives and drawn them irresistibly toward their Lord.

Jesus knew that Judas was primed by the devil to betray Him, but rather than preparing a defense or an alibi, Jesus prepared His disciples to counter the betrayal and hatred that would surely follow them with love and humility. The world is still thrown off by this strategy and does not know how to respond when the Christian presents a Messiah who returns love for hate. This principle has been the foundation of non-violent, nonaggressive strategies for change since Jesus walked the earth, and it is incredibly disarming. With this act of foot washing, Jesus raised the bar by lowering the bar.

During this final meal, after Jesus gave instructions on how the disciples were to commemorate the Lord's supper (Luke 22:14-22), the disciples began to discuss who was the greatest. Jesus doubled down on teaching humility. Jesus explained that kings and gentiles lord their authority over the masses, but His disciples were to be different. Jesus explained that His disciples were to be servant leaders who are not above those whom they lead. (Luke 22:24-27). After the last supper, Jesus went to the Garden of Gethsemane to pray, and here He taught His disciples another difficult lesson. Having taught His disciples about the power of humility, the lesson Jesus taught in the garden was a lesson about defending themselves and their ministries.

Betrayed With A Kiss

Human beings are instinctively defensive, and we can see it in the way we respond to adversity in our lives. The ideas of loving our enemies and turning the other cheek are counterintuitive for us. During His earthly ministry, Jesus was breaking down and dismantling the institutions of His disciples, and in the previous section, we saw an example of this when Jesus washed the feet of His disciples. After the last supper, Judas left to put into motion the plan given to him by the devil. Judas gathered a large crowd armed with clubs and swords to arrest Jesus along with His disciples.

When Judas saw Jesus in the garden, he approached and kissed Him as was the prearranged signal to the crowd. Jesus responded by saying, "***Are you betraying the Son of Man with a kiss***?" Jesus did not order His disciples to fight their way out of the situation, nor did He pray to His father to dispatch legions of angels to come to His defense. When one of the disciples drew his sword and cut off the ear of the High Priest's slave, Jesus said, "***Stop, no more of this.***" Jesus then healed the injured slave. (Luke 47:51) In Matthew's gospel, we read where Jesus said, "***Put your sword back into its place; for all those who take up the sword shall perish by***

the sword. Or do you think that I cannot appeal to My father, and He will at once put at My disposal more than twelve legions of angels?" (Matthew 47:52-53) Jesus was not teaching that Christians should always remain defenseless, but He was teaching that taking direct and immediate action often denies the opportunity for God to do what He does in the spiritual realm, and that demonstrable love is more powerful and effective than the sword.

I think this lesson of non-defensiveness is one that Jesus is still teaching His disciples (Christians) today. The Christian response to opposition is often just as pugilistic as that of the world. When Christians feel the church is under attack, our natural response is to fight back. We are inclined to fight back legally, on social media, politically, and in any other way we can justify. We take on abortion and a handful of other social, political, and legal issues. Our response as a church has been to align ourselves with a political party in order to fight these issues with manmade laws, much like using clubs and swords. The 7th commandment is that we are not to commit adultery, which Jesus describes as a precursor to divorce (Matthew 5:31-32), yet even within the Christian church, the first thing we tend to say to someone who is facing divorce is to get a lawyer and protect your assets. I wonder how the world would respond if the church followed the example Jesus set, to humble ourselves, love the lost, and drop our defenses rather than raise our swords.

The full impact of what Jesus did in the garden was not and could not have been experienced by the disciples until after Jesus was crucified and raised from the dead. By this time, the disciples had seen Jesus do so many mind-boggling things like turning water into wine, feeding 5,000 with a few fish and a few loaves of bread, healing the sick, giving sight to the blind, and raising the dead. However, demonstrating the power of this lesson, which is that love coupled with faith had to run its course, it had to wait until He had been crucified. This delayed impact is what landed on the disciples after the resurrection. Understanding that Jesus could have fought off the mob with legions of angels, yet He chose the non-defensive path would have drawn His disciples closer to Him after the resurrection, and it should draw us close to Him as well. We should also learn the futility of taking up arms against our enemies and the power of trusting in our Savior.

The Cost Of Discipleship

At some point, most of us experience the sheer joy of making an unbelievable deal on something of great value. Getting a great deal involves knowing the value of your potential acquisition and realizing when it is being offered at a price that is nearly impossible to beat. In her 1958 book, *Shadow of Almighty,* Elisabeth Elliot wrote of the life and martyrdom of her first husband, Jim Elliot, who was killed along with Pete Fleming, Ed McCully, Nate Saint, and Roger Youderian in 1956 during a missionary journey to the Waodani people of Ecuador. In her book, Elisabeth published notes written by her husband, and one of the most intriguing quotes from these writings is his statement, "*He is no fool who gives what he cannot keep in order to gain what he can never lose*".

The Waodani were a non-trusting, violent, and paranoid tribal people known for resolving conflict by spearing their enemies to death. Although the missionary group had made some significant progress during their initial outreach, at one point it became clear that circumstances had become extremely dangerous and that violence was inevitable. Equipped with firearms that could have saved their lives, the missionaries had already agreed that while they were ready to die, the Waodani were not. Therefore, they decided to only use the guns to fire into the air and hopefully scare the Waodani off, but they would not kill them. As a result, all five men were speared to death.

Jim Elliot and the other missionaries understood the high cost of discipleship as well as its high reward. In 2005, the movie, "*End of the Spear*" was released. The movie chronicles the journey of Steve Saint, who is the son of missionary pilot Nate Saint. Nate is one of the missionaries who was killed by the Waodani during the 1956 missionary journey to Ecuador. As an adult, Steve Saint returned with his family to the jungles of Ecuador to bury his aunt Rachel, who had successfully established relations with the Waodani and lived with them since shortly after her brother, Nate, was killed by them. The movie, End of the Spear, describes how the early work of Steve's father, Nate, along with the other missionaries, paved the way for the eventual conversion of the men who killed them.

The early disciples had their own idea of what it meant to follow the Messiah prophesied in Old Testament scripture, and it is unlikely these disciples initially understood that following Jesus would cost them so much. To prepare His disciples for what was to come, Jesus needed to adjust their expectations, and the same is true for us as 21st-century believers. Until we reach a point where we understand and expect our relationship with Jesus to cost us everything, we are not ready to truly be His disciples. Reading through the gospels and then through the book of Acts, we can see that in time, the disciples did clearly understand the cost of following Jesus. Having become intimately familiar with the scriptures, Jim Elliot and his fellow missionaries also understood the high cost of following Jesus.

I have mentioned Matthew 10:34 previously in this book because I find Jesus' words in this verse extremely shocking. This verse has an important application now as we discuss the cost of being a follower of Jesus. In an effort to explain the high cost of being a true follower, Jesus said in this passage, "***Do not think that I came to bring peace on the earth; I did not come to bring peace, but a sword, For I came to set a man against his father, and a daughter against her mother, and a daughter-in-law against her mother-in-law; and a man's enemies will be the members of his household. He who loves father or mother more than Me is not worthy of Me; and he who loves son or daughter more than Me is not worthy of Me. And he who does not take his cross and follow after me is not worthy of Me. He who has found his life will lose it, and he who has lost his life for My sake will find it.***" I believe this is one of the most challenging yet important passages of Jesus's teaching that needs to be understood and fully embraced by every Christian.

Most people who follow Jesus have experienced the truth of Matthew 10:34-39 to one degree or another, and it is essential for us to embrace the fact that this is all part of the plan. The Apostle Peter, who was eventually crucified upside down for his faith demonstrated his understanding of the high cost of being a disciple in what he wrote, ***"Beloved, do not be surprised at the fiery ordeal among you, which comes upon you for your testing, as though some strange thing were happening to you; but to the degree that you share in the sufferings of Christ, keep on rejoicing, so that***

***also at the revelation of His glory you may rejoice with exultation*.**" (1 Peter 4:12-13)

Following Jesus can certainly cost a person their lives, as was the case with Jim Elliot and the other missionaries with him, as well as countless missionaries throughout history, but it often costs the believer precious relationships with family, friends, and within their communities. One of the most destructive heresies of modern, Western Christianity is the notion that the Bible is a book written to bring us comfort or that Christianity provides protection from harm. A full commitment to following Jesus can cost you everything you hold dear in this life, yet by making this commitment, one will find indescribable joy in this life and in the life to come.

As Jesus walked toward Jerusalem with His disciples, He knew what was going to happen to Him. Jesus told the disciples that He would be delivered to the chief priests and the scribes and that eventually He would be killed. Having just told the men what was about to happen to Him, John and James asked Jesus if one of them could sit on His right and left side in His glory. Realizing that they missed the point Jesus was teaching about discipleship, and that they did not understand what was about to happen both to Himself and to His disciples, Jesus took the opportunity to explain. (Mark 10:32-45)

In His discourse with the disciples during this walk to Jerusalem, Jesus used words and imagery to disrupt their carnal expectations of what it meant to be a disciple of the Messiah. Theirs would not be a life of luxury or of condescension. Rather than ruling from a position of lofty comfort, Jesus explained that leadership meant service and sacrifice, and that ultimately, they would be called to give their very lives just as He eventually would. This unvarnished truth weighed heavily on the disciples and forced them to reimagine their futures. It is only through this transformation of their minds (Romans 12:1) that they and we become useful in Christian ministry.

As we imagine being in the sandals of those who walked alongside our Lord and Savior, we need only examine their lives pre- and post-crucifixion. The lessons Jesus taught about leadership were fresh, and they were a radical departure from the status quo. No one had ever heard the things Jesus said, and no one had ever seen the things done that Jesus did; not just the miracles, but His commitment to both live and die for the world He loved. Jesus set the standard for leadership during His earthly ministry, and everyone around Him knew they were witnessing something incredible. I encourage you to discover the lessons of leadership taught by Jesus for yourself but do so by inserting yourself into the context of being a first-century Jew. The things Jesus said and did would have been the subject of conversations in each synagogue and in every household of those who walked with Him. The leadership perspectives of each person Jesus encountered were forever altered.

As I close this segment and this chapter, I want to share a brief story. Years ago, someone whom I cared very much for told me about how they had left a religious cult and that, as a result, their entire family turned their backs on them. My friend grieved the loss of relationships with their beloved family, and it angered my friend that the transition meant being disowned by their only brother. Sometime later, as this friend reflected on the loss, it became apparent that while their new faith cost them relationships with natural family members, God provided them with many brothers within the Christian community. Being a disciple is costly, but regardless of how things look in the immediate term, as Jim Elliot put it, gaining what we can never lose in exchange for that which we can never keep is always a deal well worth taking.

Chapter Five

Friend

Defining Friendship

The phrase, Jesus is a friend of mine, is often used in Christian parlance and in Christian worship music. However, it is important to consider what this phrase means to the modern believer, and what it meant to be counted as a friend of Jesus to those who walked with Him during His time on earth. In this chapter, we will consider what the followers of Jesus witnessed and experienced as they developed a friendship with Jesus, and how He let those around Him know that His friendship was sacrificial, without boundaries, deep, abiding, and eternal. We will examine how this facet of Jesus's being was revealed to others and what it might mean for us to experience friendship with Jesus in our own lives.

Friendship is a term that has become so watered down that we need to deconstruct what we believe about the term and reconstruct its meaning based upon what Jesus taught and what He modeled. Jesus is the ultimate pedagogue. His method of teaching, followed by demonstrable actions, is on full display as He led His disciples toward a full, unadulterated understanding of what it means to be a friend.

Jesus said, "***This is My commandment, that you love one another, just as I have loved you. Greater love has no one than this, that one lay down his life for his friends***." (John 15:12-13) In John chapter 15, verses 12-17, Jesus does not make suggestions or recommendations; He is issuing commands. The word command is used three times in these verses, the word friend is used three times, and the word “love" is used four times. Therefore, as we look at what it meant to be a friend of Jesus, it seems prudent that we have a firm grasp on what Jesus taught and what He demonstrated about the connection between friendship and love.

Jesus told His disciples that the greatest manifestation of love is that a person lay down their life for their friends. When we think about laying down our lives, most often we think about dying for someone or something. Death is the final human experience that each person must face, but life is ongoing. I wonder how it might change our perspective on what Jesus said if we broaden our concept of what He meant. Yes, laying down one’s life can certainly mean dying for someone or for something, but it can also mean living for someone or something. Martyrs are few and far between. All the apostles except John were martyred, and we may also have to die for our faith and for our friends. However, consider the difference we can make for our friends, family, and the world if we choose to live for Christ so that we can minister to those whom we love.

Jesus also told His disciples that evidence of their friendship with Him would be that they obey His commandments. I meet people all the time who say they are Christians, and then when I ask them when they last read their Bible, they cannot recall. I have also met Christians who are not even sure if they own a Bible. My point is this: being a friend of Jesus means, among other things, obedience. To be obedient, one must know what they are being commanded to do. In a Christian context, this means reading and seeking to understand the scriptures.

Jesus went on to explain to His disciples that as friends, they were not to consider themselves slaves or automatons, knowing nothing about why they were doing that which they were commanded to do. Jesus said He would reveal what He is doing to them because they were more than slaves, they were friends. This again requires that we hear His voice, which requires both prayer and consistent reading of His Word. (John 15:14)

Experiencing Friendship

While in high school, I became enamored with a classmate of mine who was a phenomenal pianist. Between class periods and during breaks in our schedules, I would go to the band room where there was a piano, and I would watch him play all sorts of interesting chord progressions. Every now and then, I would ask him to show me some of the chord progressions he used, and he would patiently show me how to mimic what he was doing; sometimes he would even place his hands over mine, take my fingers. and put them on the keys where they needed to be. When I missed a note or played something incorrectly, he would just smile at me disarmingly and say, "*No, Doug, that's wrong, do it the way I showed you.*" Although I knew he was right, his words wounded me because I wanted so much to impress him. He was my peer, and he was correcting me, telling me that the way I was going about playing the chords was wrong. However, it was impossible for me to get angry with him because I knew his only reason for correcting me was so that I would learn the right way to play the chords. The fact is, he really wanted me to do well.

Proverbs 27:6 reads, "***Faithful are the wounds of a friend, but deceitful are the kisses of an enemy.***" Although I never became a great pianist, my friend did, and the wounds he inflicted on me in that choir room made me a more disciplined musician, a better learner, and a better version of myself for the rest of my life. My friend could never have had the impact on me that he did by telling me I was playing the chords correctly when I was not. I will always look back on the precious moments I spent with him with gratitude, because his friendship added so much value to my life. This, I believe, is a picture of how Jesus would have been seen by those whom He considered his close friends. Jesus was firm, direct, and His intention was unmistakable. Jesus was investing in the future value of His friend's lives through His loving guidance. As we reflect on the passages which highlight Jesus as a friend, I urge you to keep in mind the example I gave of my high school friend, or better yet, consider time you have spent with a true friend in your own life; perhaps a friend who loved you enough to insist that you got things right and that you become the best that you can be.

The Intimacy Of Friendship

One of the characteristics of friendship is that friends are aware of information about each other that those who are not in our friendship circles are not aware of. There are things I do and say that only those whom I consider friends have enough information about me to understand; others who hear what I say or witness what I do can only scratch their heads and wonder what I am thinking. This is especially true for childhood friendships.

When we are young, we tend to seek out trusted relationships with people outside our immediate family, but we often develop close friendships within it. Jesus had a very public ministry wherein He made bold proclamations to the masses, and it was not uncommon for the multitudes to struggle with understanding what He had said in His parables and other statements. However, Jesus wanted His close inner circle to be free from ambiguity regarding His teachings. This inner circle of friends had the inside scoop.

Jesus told parables so those listening could actively engage with the subject He was teaching. In the process, Jesus used images that would be easy for them to grasp. While the listener would have to work through the meaning of a parable, everything they needed to work out the meaning was available to them. These parables were intended to compel the listener to apply the knowledge they already possessed to the revelation He provided within the parable. As much as Jesus knew it would take time for the masses to reason through what He said, Jesus wanted His disciples to grasp these concepts without delay, because as His time on earth was drawing to a close, it was the men in His inner circle who would eventually proliferate the gospel to the entire world. For this reason, Jesus gave His inner circle the answers to the test.

Having just taught the parable of the Sower who sowed seed beside the road, and on rocky ground, among thorns, and then on good soil, Jesus wanted His inner circle to understand what this parable meant, even if the masses would struggle to understand His message. When He was alone with these men, they began asking Him about the parable, at which point, Jesus spelled out the meaning in unambiguous terms. (Mark 4:1-20) These disciples were sanctified, or set apart, for the mission they were about to be sent on, and Jesus was turning disciples into apostles.

Jesus washed the disciples' feet during the last supper, and when He finished, He made two proclamations. The first proclamation was that these men would be an essential part of His ministry as emissaries, and that anyone who listened to these men was listening to and learning from Him. The second proclamation was that one of these men would betray Him. (John 13:20-26) I invite you to consider this bifurcated proclamation from the following perspective.

After Jesus told His disciples that they would speak for Him, He said that one of them would betray Him. These two statements were not mutually exclusive; in fact, they were two sides of the same coin. At the same time, Jesus told His disciples they had been given a divine destiny. He also declared that for one of them, Judas, this blessed destiny was not enough. In this moment, Jesus framed the human dilemma that continued to play out from that moment until this very hour. The problem with Judas was not singular or specific to one man; it is emblematic of the entire human race. Our nature is to betray Jesus by dismissing Him as insufficient, and this truth grieved Jesus deep in His Spirit. However, Jesus also understands that the cross is the only cure for our compromised nature.

The original twelve disciples, eleven of whom eventually became apostles, had a connection with Jesus that drew them into a deeper relationship with Him. The revelation that one of them would betray Jesus was like a gut punch to the other faithful disciples. Although no one inside that room would have understood the magnitude of what Jesus was saying until after the crucifixion, Peter and John wanted the inside scoop; they wanted to know who would betray the Lord. To gain full details of what Jesus had said, Peter leaned in close to John as he reclined, laying his head on the chest of Jesus, and Peter told John to ask Jesus who would betray Him. Jesus answered their question.

Although the rest of the world was caught off guard by Judas's betrayal and the eventual crucifixion of Jesus, none of this came as a surprise to the closest friends of Jesus because He told them what would happen in advance. These men knew what was happening, and this knowledge better prepared them for the ministry they would soon inherit. To understand the impact this had on the disciples, think of how it might affect you if you had been reclining at the table with Jesus during the last supper and He confided in you that He would be killed. Consider how it would have affected you if Jesus identified the betrayer, and the events unfolded exactly as He predicted. In the moment when the betrayal occurred, aside from fear and anger, you would probably feel trusted and loved by Jesus because He had decided to confide in you, and it might deepen your intimacy with your friend, the Savior.

Prevenient Grace

Following the last supper, a discussion arose among the disciples. So much had occurred in a single night: Jesus washed the feet of His disciples, He proclaimed that they would embark upon a mission to preach the gospel, and He revealed that one of them would betray Him. After all of this, they began to discuss who would be the greatest in the Kingdom. (Luke 22:24-34) Jesus patiently laid out the principles of servant leadership, and then He abruptly turned His attention to Peter, saying, "***Simon, Simon, behold, Satan has demanded permission to sift you like wheat.***" This passage of scripture reminds us that anytime we come under attack from Satan, he has to ask and be granted permission by God, and that God uses these attacks for His divine purpose. (Job 1:6-12)

Apparently, God the Father granted Satan permission to test Peter, but in this passage, Jesus said something amazing that is easily overlooked. Jesus said, "***But I have prayed for you,***

that your faith may not fail; and you, when once you have turned again, strengthen your brothers."

Prevenient grace is a theological term most often used to refute the Calvinist doctrine of unconditional election. Without getting too far into the theological weeds, Calvinism or reformed theology says that salvation is a matter of predestined election, and that we play absolutely no role in our own salvation. On the other hand, Methodists and some other faith traditions believe in prevenient grace, which precedes conversion and provides a pathway to salvation by God's grace, which intercedes on our behalf and enables a person to choose salvation. I am using the term prevenient grace here not to describe a method of salvation but to describe the grace Jesus extended to Peter despite His foreknowledge that Peter would deny Him.

In Luke 22:31-32, Jesus told Peter that he would fail, but more importantly, Jesus prayed that when Peter did fail, he would return to the faith stronger than when he began. Jesus prayed that Peter would use the strength he would acquire through his failure to strengthen his brothers. This is the essence of prevenient grace! Knowing that Peter would fail, Jesus extended grace to him, even in advance of his imminent failure. This is a powerful message for us as followers of Jesus who know that Satan continually asks to sift us like wheat. Satan is always seeking an opportunity to destroy us, but God continues to use the devil's mischief to move His own agenda forward. (John 10:10, 1 Peter 5:8, Genesis 50:20). We can therefore rest assured that our failures, even those brought on by the evil intentions of the enemy, will not prevail against the plan of God, and He will use our failure to thwart the plans of Satan.

I can only imagine that Jesus must have smiled at Peter's response when He told Peter he would stumble. Peter probably saw the indictment in Jesus's prediction, but he did not see the grace being extended to him. Peter did not see that Jesus was telling him he would be made stronger because of his failure. Having missed all of this, Peter went right to defending himself and declaring that he was ready to go both to prison and to his death for Jesus, but scripture tells us how that turned out. (John 19:25-27) Peter must have been overcome with an incredible awareness of Jesus's love for him as he stood in the courtyard hearing the rooster crow after he had twice denied Him. These were the moments that set the stage for the dialogue between Jesus and Peter by the seashore. (John 21:15-17)

The Faithful Wound

Baltasar Gracian, a Spanish Jesuit priest, once wrote, "*Friendship multiplies the good of life and divides the evil.*" I love the confluence of math and poetry embedded within this heartwarming description of friendship. It is true that a friend bears the burdens of life while infusing it with joy, so I wholeheartedly agree with the sentiment conveyed in this quote. To finish this chapter, I want to look at a lesson Jesus teaches us on how love and friendship go hand in hand. In this lesson, Jesus uses a conversation between Himself and Peter to teach us that love is revealed not in what we say but in what we do.

After the resurrection, Jesus and His disciples met by the seashore. (John 21). When we read chapter 21 of John's gospel, we are presented with a Peter who, after jumping into the water to get to the shore and greet his Lord, appears somewhat sheepish. Perhaps Peter was feeling the weight of his failure after denying Jesus during His trial. Jesus, however, would not allow Peter to shrink into the shadows. He beckoned Peter out of obscurity and into prominence with a compelling call to the ultimate expression of friendship.

In the previous section, we looked at the encounter between Jesus and Peter, which took place after Jesus had washed the feet of His disciples and predicted Judas's betrayal. During this conversation, Jesus also told Peter that he was going to stumble because God had given Satan permission to cause him to stumble. Jesus had grand plans for Peter, but before Jesus could use Peter the way He wanted to, Jesus had to allow Peter to be broken, not destroyed, but broken. Peter needed to see the natural man within himself for the spiritual man to be fully revealed. Peter needed to be brought from hubris to humility, and Satan was the instrument Jesus used to accomplish this purpose.

Jesus told Peter that before the rooster crowed, he would deny Him three times, but due to his own hubris, Peter could not imagine the possibility of failing to stand strong for his Lord. Jesus needed to hold a mirror up to Peter's face so that He could reveal Peter's weakness. Only by acknowledging his natural weakness could Peter's spiritual strength emerge. Jesus never berated Peter for stumbling, but He needed Peter to be aware of it, and the best way to reveal this weakness was through the experience (Being sifted by Satan), which God the Father allowed to play out during the trial of Jesus. This is a perfect example of Proverbs 27:6. "***Faithful are the wounds of a friend, but deceitful are the kisses of an enemy***" The faithful wounds of Jesus [***<u>The look from Jesus after Peter denied Him</u>***] were far more precious than the deceitful kisses from an enemy could ever be. To bring out the very best in Peter, Jesus allowed him to experience the very worst, that of being wounded by his friend, savior, and Lord.

Remember what happened after Peter denied Jesus for the third time? Jesus looked at him, and in that moment, Peter remembered Jesus had predicted what would happen. (Luke 54-64) I do not imagine Jesus's facial expression was one of condemnation, triumph, or even sarcasm, I imagine Jesus's look conveyed understanding, love, friendship, and forgiveness. In that moment, Peter understood what he was capable of in his humanity, but through this experience, he eventually understood the grace of his Lord and Savior, and he went out weeping bitterly. After experiencing this moment of failure, Peter began to transform from the disciple he had been, into the apostle he was to become.

As the men gathered by the seashore, enjoying company with Jesus over a breakfast of broiled fish, Jesus approached Peter and three times He asked Peter if he loved Him. The limitations of the English language make it somewhat challenging to fully capture the significance of this conversation. The first two times Jesus asked Peter if he loved Him, Jesus used the Greek word agape, which is the highest form of love. Peter responded by acknowledging that he loved Jesus, but Peter used the Greek word Philéo, which is an affectionate term for love that conveys friendship or brotherly love. The final time Jesus asked Peter if he loved Him, Jesus used the word Philéo, and Peter, having seen himself reflected in the mirror, responded by confirming that he did not yet love Jesus as he ought to and as he wanted to by again affirming that his love for Jesus was not agape, but Philéo.

Now that Jesus has allowed Peter to experience failure, He could begin to build Peter up because Peter had dropped all pretense and was no longer building himself up. These are the faithful wounds of a friend in action, used to help someone become who they were meant to become. This is what Jesus will do for us if we let Him. He will hold that mirror up to our face and reveal who we are as human beings so that we can emerge into spiritual beings that He can use for His purpose.

Chapter Six

Teacher

Jesus was called rabbi, but His message was unique in style, delivery, and content. Although forty-two percent of Mark's gospel mentions Jesus's teaching, the main emphasis of is to present Jesus as the suffering servant. As we look into how those around Jesus would have experienced Him as their teacher, Mark gives us an important insight into this facet of Jesus. In Mark 1:22, we read, "***They were amazed at His teaching; for He was teaching them as one having authority and not as the scribes***." Mark uses the word authority in this verse to distinguish between the scribes, who leaned on the wisdom of others to lend veracity to their own suppositions, and Jesus, whose wisdom and lines of thought were original.

We live in the information age, and although I'm not sure we are getting more information than we used to, we are getting information faster, and it comes from greater distances and more sources than it did in the 1st century. However, the desire of people to see or hear the latest spin on the questions of life is pretty much the same. As we move through this chapter, I want us to consider that although the people living in the ancient near east during the first century heard from several teachers, we want to know what made Jesus different. We want to know why people flocked to Him then, and why are we still amazed at what He taught. Mark 1:22 offers us valuable insight into this question.

Some of the most rewarding times of my life have been spent teaching on a college campus. I learned early on that teaching is all about using the knowledge the student already has to connect them with knowledge they do yet have. Put another way, effective teaching is more about expanding the information a person already has than simply presenting them with new information.

Stories create connections between concepts and information a person already understands and concepts they do not yet understand. Think about a favorite teacher in your life, and more than likely, you will realize that the teacher you have in mind raptured your attention by telling relatable stories and anecdotes with the lesson they wanted you to learn embedded within those stories. Even math and science teachers leverage the power of short stories to make otherwise difficult concepts more accessible to the student. When I lectured, and I saw my students' attention begin to wane, the best way to regain their attention was by telling a story that related to the material I was teaching.

Jesus used parables (Stories) to create understanding by taking concepts that anyone listening to him could relate to and using those concepts, which they already understood, to connect them with the truth they did not yet understand and were not yet living. In His parables, Jesus would often take Old Testament scriptures that were commonly known but had been misapplied over the centuries. Jesus used agricultural concepts and other examples common to daily 1st century life to make a point. Much of what Jesus said was pedagogical, but in this chapter, we will focus on the content of His lessons, the methods He used to teach, and the impact His teaching had on those to whom He spoke.

Our goal will be to discover what the followers of Jesus witnessed and experienced about His style of teaching. We will discover what it meant to have Jesus as a teacher, and how Jesus' teaching was different than that of any other rabbi. We want to know how Jesus explained scripture and life in ways that no one else had done, and what made the things Jesus taught different from those of others who were making a name for themselves during this time.

Before we dig in, I want to offer a distinction between teaching and preaching. For the sake of this chapter and the next, I will define teaching as the method used by one person to develop understanding and expand knowledge in another person. Preaching, which will be our topic for chapter seven, is didactic oration that moves beyond conventional wisdom and elucidates the Word of God for the purpose of motivating people to think and to live differently.

The teachings of Jesus have had a more powerful effect on human history than anything before or after His three-year earthly ministry. We will discuss the methods used by Jesus to teach on the topics of:

- Love:
    - John 3:16
    - John 15:13 Sacrifice
    - Matthew 22:36-40
    - John 21:15-17
- Law:
    - John 8:1-11
    - Matthew 15:1-11
- Christian Living:
    - Mark 4:13-22
    - Mark 10:17-31
    - Mark 12:41-44
    - Luke 7:37-47
    - Luke 10:25-37

It would not make sense to look at what Jesus taught without first examining His prolific use of parables to challenge the thinking of His followers. Of course, we cannot do an in-depth study of all the parables Jesus used, but we will get into the way Jesus used parables in Matthew 13, where He was particularly clever about explaining life-changing principles:

Matthew 13

The disciples asked Jesus why He spoke to the people in parables, and He answered them. Like many of you, I have read Matthew 13:17 many times, and it seemed to me that Jesus was almost being dismissive of the crowd by speaking in parables rather than speaking to them plainly. It appeared that Jesus did not value them as He valued His inner circle of disciples. Upon close inspection, I see that Jesus was actually trying to bless the crowd by helping them develop a discipline of understanding principles rather than simple rules.

Jesus was encouraging them to develop and exercise their ability to think and to reason rather than waiting to be spoon-fed all the answers. Jesus understood that in reality, there may have been many reasons for the crowd to have gathered around Him, but whatever their reasons, they were not actively seeking truth. The disciples asked Jesus why he spoke in parables as if it was His responsibility to make the crowd understand, but it was not.

Jesus explained to His disciples that He spoke to the crowd in parables because although they had been given vision, they do not use their God-given vision to see, and although they had been given the ability to hear, they did not use their God-given ability to hear, listen, and understand. (Matthew 13:10-13). When you read these verses, notice that Jesus did not say they cannot see or hear; he said they do not see or hear. This simple distinction informs us that, whereas the crowd was given everything they needed for comprehension, they chose ignorance. The disciples, on the other hand, used their God-given faculties to seek out wisdom and to apply themselves to understanding. This was demonstrated by their commitment to leave the comfort of their families and businesses to follow Jesus and sit at His feet to learn.

There is a Taoist quote that is often mistakenly ascribed to Christian doctrine, which says, "*Give a man a fish, and you feed him for a day. Teach him how to fish, and you feed him for a lifetime.*" Although there is no Biblical record of Jesus ever uttering these words, Matthew 13:10-17 is an example of Jesus demonstrating the principle that when you give someone what they need, it is used or consumed, but the means to acquire it is not obtained by the beneficiary. When I rely on someone else over and over again to show me how to do something, eventually, they will be rightfully exasperated with my complacency. If that person loves me, they will teach me how to do it myself so that I am learning new skills and I am developing my capacity to contribute to my own growth. Having learned a new skill, I can then pass this knowledge on to others.

This phenomenon is still observable today. The masses, whether outside the church or, unfortunately, even within the church, wait passively to be enlightened or to have knowledge impressed upon them, usually through the most entertaining medium. In conversations with people outside the Christian faith, rather than listening to understand what unsaved people are saying, and presenting a loving, winsome explanation of the gospel, we tend to respond with harsh words of condemnation as if the goal were to win an argument.

Many of the people we encounter outside the faith who have a fully formed opinion about Christianity have never opened the Bible, and it is difficult to correct their errors because too often we are unwilling to read the Bible, read good books on Christian history, doctrine, or theology, to better understand Jesus and His gospel ourselves. This is the crowd that gathered around Jesus; they were more than willing to hear something that confirmed their religious beliefs, which they took little or no effort to understand or live out, but Jesus loved them too much to let them off the hook that easily. Jesus presented messages that required them to use their God-given faculties to comprehend and principles that challenged the way they lived their lives.

Jesus was a master communicator, and those in the crowd around Him could easily relate to and understand the examples He used in His parables. Even if the message itself was challenging to their worldview and lifestyle, the information was presented in ways that made the lessons He taught accessible to them. If you enjoy reading parables, the Gospel of Luke is a rich source for finding many of the parables Jesus told. However, in Matthew 13, Jesus did a masterful job of tapping into the knowledge the crowd already possessed for the sake of developing their understanding of key concepts they may never have considered.

Jesus used themes relating to agriculture, the fishing industry, and even treasure hunting, to teach them about kingdom living:

- Sowing (Planting) – Matthew 13:3-9

- Tares and wheat – Matthew 13:24-30
- The mustard seed – Matthew 13:31
- Leaven – Matthew 13:33
- Finding Pearls – Matthew 13:45
- Fishing – Matthew 13:47-51

Each of the above parables was easy to understand in principle, but the wisdom hidden within the parables was not. Seen in this light, we understand there was nothing lacking in the approach Jesus used to teach, and they had everything they needed to grasp the concepts He taught, but there was a lack of will to accept the truth of His message. Wisdom is always accessible in the Word of God, but so often our desire for sin tends to overcomplicate the simplicity of what Jesus teaches. Our own stubbornness can therefore frustrate our ability to comprehend the truth of the Gospel.

As Jesus spoke in parables, those among His inner circle had never been taught such incredible truth in such a compelling way. Those who sought truth and had committed their lives to following Jesus were awestruck. Like everyone else, they knew there was something lacking in the law and they knew there was no life-transforming power in what was taught by the Pharisees, the Sadducees, and the Scribes; but in Jesus, they found truth, love, and life. The parables Jesus used were an essential component of their learning process, and the impact on their lives was absolute. All of this is still true today. We can and we should seek knowledge in books and in the university, but nothing in the 1st century or in the 21st century has the capacity to upend our lives and change us from the inside out like the ministry of Jesus.

Love

The word love appears hundreds of times in the New Testament, most frequently in the Gospel of John. The word is often used in its verbal form, or it is used in connection with a call to action. Numerous sermons have been preached about love as a verb and many songs have been sung on the topic, but in this segment, we will look not so much at what Jesus taught about love, but how He taught about love. I will say up front that some of the most life changing lessons Jesus taught about love were in conjunction with a compelling call to action or in describing God's active love for humanity. In this segment, we will look at four scriptures, three of which are found in the Gospel of John:

- John 3:16
- John 14:6
- John 15:13
- Matthew 22:36-40

John 14:6 and 3:16

It could reasonably be argued that humanism is the antithesis of Biblical Christianity. Humanists believe that human beings are inherently good, but Biblical Christianity believes that human beings are born into sin. Therefore, whereas the humanist does not seek, nor does he require a savior, the Christian understands the dire need for a savior. The humanist might ask the question, "If there were a God, how He can allow bad things to happen to good people?" By contrast, Biblical Christianity teaches that bad things happen because we live in a fallen world, corrupted by sin, and that God is the only good in this world.

In his book, "Sinners in the hands of an angry God", eighteenth century preacher, Jonathan Edwards described humanity as being held in the hands of God over the pit of hell. Edwards reasons that all humans are destined for hell, and all would descend into hell if it were not for the love and grace of God. Having full understanding of the human dilemma, the apostle John wrote in his gospel, "***God so loved the world He gave His only begotten son, that whoever believes in Him will not perish but have everlasting life***." (John 3:16) As Christians, we understand the need for a savior, and in John 14:6 Jesus says, "***I am the way, the truth, and the life. No one comes to the Father but through me.***"

At the time Jesus made the audacious John 14:6 statement, no one understood that our path to the Father required Jesus to willingly offer His own life to atone for our sins, but in retrospect, we can see now that Jesus was drawing a direct connection between His future sacrifice, and the availability of salvation, purchased by the demonstrable love of the Father. John 14:6 rolls off the tongue so easily and smoothly that it's helpful to break it down into its four constituent statements. In this verse Jesus declares that He is:

1. The way
2. The truth
3. The life
4. The exclusive means of reaching God

John 14:6 was spoken by Jesus, to His inner circle of disciples and none of them had ever heard words like this before. When Jesus called the disciples, they had been awaiting a messiah, but they had in mind someone who would return them to their pre-exilic existence where the Jews were a self-governing nation. Through spending time with Jesus, they learned to think of salvation in terms of a messiah who would lead them in spiritual reformation and restore their relationship with God. With His statement in John 14:6, Jesus declared that He is the conduit between them and a restored relationship with the sovereign God of the universe.

The precursor to John 14:6 is John 14:5 where Thomas asked Jesus how they would know where He was going. In response to this question Jesus said, "***I am the way***", letting them know they needed to follow Him. By saying "***I am the truth***", Jesus let them know that His words and His teaching were the standard for righteousness. By saying "***I am the life***", Jesus was letting them know that the key to eternal life was vested in Him alone. By saying "***No one comes to the father but through Me***", Jesus was letting them know that anyone wishing to be reconciled to God needed to be reconciled with Him.

John 3:16 tells us that God so loved the world, He gave His only begotten Son, but Jesus, the Son of God, tells us in John 14:6 that out of an abundance of God's love for us, He has been given to us as a conduit to the Father. The religious authorities of the day taught piety by works of the law; Jesus taught salvation as a manifestation of God's love. Although none of the disciples listening to Jesus speak that day understood that coming to the Father would mean Jesus giving up His life, they did understand that Jesus was teaching them that there is a direct connection between the love we feel and the actions associated with love. It might help to look at these two scriptures like this: John 3:16 is the proclamation of God's love, and John 14:6 is the manifestation of that love.

John 15:13

The word connection is used frequently these days as people seek greater and more meaningful relationships. This quest for connection should cause us to question how it can be that we live in a world where, within seconds, we can see and speak with a loved one who lives on the other side of the planet, yet so many people continue to strive for the connection we humans so desperately crave. It is an interesting paradox that while we long for connection, independence is often associated with success.

From Genesis through Revelation, the Bible points toward the connection between husband and wife, parent and child, God and humanity, and within the Holy Trinity itself. If you look for it, you can see a picture of symbiosis throughout the Bible. In John chapter 15, Jesus gives a masterful lesson on connectivity using love and obedience as the primary ingredients.

As a writer, I am always conscious of repeating words excessively, but when we see repetition in the Bible, it's a good idea for us to pay attention to what God is trying to tell us. Between John 13:1 and John 15:13, the word love is used 8 times as Jesus describes the connections between the Father, the Son, the Holy Spirit, and humanity.

The connective tissue between these relationships is love as demonstrated by what we do and our willingness to be obedient. The conceptual framework for what Jesus taught is unique. It is not uncommon for people to expect acquiescence as proof of someone's love for them, and at first glance, that's what it appears Jesus is doing in John 15:10. However, when we look closer, we see that is not what Jesus is doing. Jesus did not say, " If you love me, you will keep my commandments; rather, Jesus said, " If you keep my commandments, you will abide (Continue or endure) in My love. Put another way, Jesus is saying that keeping His commandments will empower us to persist in loving Him and loving others. Obeying His commandment, therefore, is not a way of proving our love for Jesus; obeying

His commandments enables us to love. Jesus was building up to His main point, which is the sacrificial nature of love.

Jesus knows that sacrificial love was then and is now very counterintuitive for us. If we relegate love to how we feel, it costs us nothing and benefits very little, but when we love with a sacrificial heart, it costs us everything, and the benefits are immeasurable. Before reaching the pinnacle of His teaching on love, Jesus gave us the formula for success; obey His commandments, and we will be able to love sacrificially. In verse 13, Jesus drops the bomb as he says, "***Greater love has no one than this, that one laydown his life for his friends***." Throughout this discourse, Jesus hints that He will eventually sacrifice His life for them and for all humanity. Of course, we know the story of the cross, but His disciples didn't have that story yet.

Most of my life, I thought John 15:13 meant that as a Christian I needed to be prepared to die as Jesus died so that others could live. In chapter four of this book, we touched on the missionaries who went to Ecuador and eventually allowed themselves to be martyred. I realize that someday, standing for the faith may require any Christian to die for the sake of the gospel. However, I also think it is important to consider that sometimes laying down one's life is not about dying, it's about living a life of undeterred faith. Each of the disciples who heard Jesus speak the words written in John 14 and 15 lived a life that demonstrated their connectedness to Jesus and a willingness to obey His commandments. This is the mission of every Christian, whether we build the church like the Apostle Peter and die a martyr's death, or live a long life of ministry ending in exile like the Apostle John.

If we study the martyrs in the Bible, beginning with Stephan in Acts 6:8 and including the Apostles and the countless followers of Jesus, we can see that while their deaths demonstrated incredible faith, their lives had the most profound effect on advancing the mission of the gospel. The notable exception to this is Jesus Himself, whose death accomplished something no other death possibly could. Therefore, it seems to me that if we want to make an impact on humanity, the emphasis should be on how we live, not how we die.

In John 15:12-13, Jesus said, "***This is My commandment, that you love one another, just as I have loved you. Greater love has no one than this, that one lay down his life for his friends***." Notice that Jesus did not say greater love has no one than that one die for his friends. To lay down one's life means to lay down or give up one's claim on one's own life. It means to cease living for oneself and begin to live for others.

The counterintuitive message of John 15:13 is that while people seek greatness in autonomy, isolation, and independence, the well-lived life involves loving others and setting aside our own agenda and selfish ambition for others. This message, given over two thousand years ago, is still shocking and counterintuitive today. We are hard-wired to be relational, connected, inter-dependent beings, yet we are inundated with messages telling us to isolate and strive for independence.

Matthew 22:36-40

Earlier in this chapter, we looked at how Jesus used parables in His teaching. In His parables, Jesus always created images that struck a chord with His listeners and helped Him drive home His point. In Matthew 22:1, Jesus told the parable of the wedding feast. In this parable, a king prepared a lavish feast for his son's wedding, and he invited all the prominent people in society to come and celebrate the wedding with him. However, none of the invited guests came to celebrate with him, and some of those he invited actually abused the messengers sent to let them know the feast was prepared. Today, if one of us is invited to a wedding, we can either accept or decline the invitation, but Jesus was describing an invitation by a king to the chosen people of a kingdom, and those listening to Him knew this was not an invitation one could simply decline because doing so would have been an incredible insult to the king.

Jesus told this parable on the heels of answering the baited questions of the religious leaders regarding taxes, which was certainly understood by the Pharisees. The Pharisees were not seeking information or opening themselves up to the teaching of Jesus; they were trying to trap Him. Jesus used the parable to tell the religious leaders that although they sat in lofty spaces within Jewish society, they had declined the invitation of God to enter His kingdom. Within the parable, Jesus went a step further by describing the consequences of someone showing up at the feast unwilling to demonstrate respect that is due to a king.

The response of Jesus to the question regarding taxes, as well as the parable of the wedding feast, created opportunities for Jesus to deflect one attack after another from those who considered themselves knowledgeable, and out of frustration and desperation, they eventually asked in Matthew 22:36, "***Teacher, which is the great commandment in the Law?***" The response Jesus gave was as powerful as it was simple, "***You shall love the Lord your God with all your heart, and with all your soul, and with all your mind. This is the great and foremost commandment. The second is like it, you shall love your neighbor as yourself. On these two***

commandments depend on the whole law and the prophets."

Therefore, the great commandment is to love God and to love others. Jesus said that everything written in the law from Genesis through Deuteronomy, and from Isaiah through Malachi, hangs together on love. This was another moment wherein Jesus laid a subtle yet potent indictment against the character and behavior of the religious leaders. They asked which is the great commandment, and Jesus told them it was the one they had not kept because they were an unloving bunch, and they had failed to meet the standard established by God which is embedded in the law and is the entire purpose of the law.

If you ever wonder why people hung on every word that came from the mouth of Jesus, remember that no one ever stood up to the religious establishment the way Jesus did. No one had ever demonstrated such a pervasive knowledge of the holy scriptures, which at the time consisted only of the law and the prophets. In addition to demonstrating great knowledge of scriptures, no one had demonstrated such an acute understanding of the deeper meaning embedded within scriptures as Jesus did. No one had been able to penetrate the hypocrisy of the Pharisees, Sadducees, and Scribes, and put them all on the defensive the way Jesus did. What Jesus did in the 1st century, He continues to do today because as a member of the body of Christ, anyone who takes the time to read and understand the Word of God has everything he/she needs to stand up to the hypocrisy of our day, and to affirm the righteous ministry of hope and love. But we must remember that Jesus was not talking about the loved one feels, and He was not talking about one's affections or preferences; Jesus was talking about demonstrable love for God and others at work in our lives as a proxy of our Savior.

Law

John 8:1-11

People are tribal by nature. We tend to stick within our groups and defend those groups fiercely, regardless of whether or not our tribe has truly taken the moral high ground. Throughout human history, we can observe an "us versus them" mentality woven into nearly every facet of our existence. Whereas we gravitate toward homogeneity, inequity, and exclusion, in His ministry, Jesus modeled diversity, equity, and inclusion. In John 8:1-11, Jesus stood on the Mount of Olives, confronted by the Scribes and Pharisees who wanted to use the Mosaic law to accuse Him. To that end, they brought Him a woman caught in adultery.

Rather than teaching a lesson specifically for the benefit of His followers, Jesus included His adversaries as beneficiaries of His wisdom and His teaching. Although the woman caught in adultery was the direct beneficiary of His actions in that moment, everyone who could hear and see Him was blessed. The religious authorities used the law to divide people into those who were compliant under their authority and those who did not conform to their narrow understanding of the law, whom they considered sinners. Jesus spoke to the religious authorities as well as everyone within earshot which included a diverse group in terms of gender, social status, and economic status, as well as those who were living outside the bubble of the religious elite.

Jesus pointed out the equity of sin. We all have an equitable share in sin because none of us, and none of them, could claim that they were without sin. It didn't take long for those who were ready to stone the woman to realize that if her sin made her a candidate for stoning, their own sin would qualify them for the same punishment. Equitable ownership in the plague of sin is one of the great constants throughout time. Therefore, the only meaningful tribes that exist are the forgiven and those who have refused to accept forgiveness.

The fact that sin equity is the bad news makes the inclusive forgiveness and salvation of Jesus such good news. Those who dropped their stones and walked away were more upset that they had lost their grounds to stone the woman and to accuse Jesus than they were excited that because the woman was forgiven of her sin, we can all be forgiven of our sins. The Pharisaic righteousness offered by the religious authorities was built on exclusivity and tribalism, but the gospel becomes even better because the only tribe one needs to belong to is the tribe that puts down their stones and drops to their knees in repentance.

Jesus directed those who wanted to find fault in the woman to look at her and see their own fault reflected in her image. Jesus did not excuse the woman's lifestyle or say that what she was doing was okay; He made her aware that grace had been extended to her despite her sin, and then He commanded her to stop sinning. This was a seminal moment for everyone gathered on the Mount of Olives that day because, for centuries, the law had been held up as the standard for morality and righteous living, but Jesus used this opportunity to demonstrate the inefficacy of the law.

Matthew 15:1-11

One of my greatest passions in life is to see more people read and seek to understand the Word of God for themselves. When I was a brand-new Christian, before I had read or studied much of the Bible, I had conversations with people who seemed to have a great command of the scriptures. They made bold and dogmatic statements about Christianity, and although the claims they made about Christianity did not resonate with what my spirit told me about the nature of God, I tended to believe them because they could quote chapter and verse, and the things they said came right out of the Bible. Over the years, I have learned that the scriptures can be twisted to mean many ungodly things when used by ungodly people with a human agenda. Even Satan is able to quote God's Word, and he has used that ability to deceive humanity since he appeared in the garden with Eve.

Jesus taught us the simplest, yet most powerful and effective response to someone who is misappropriating the Word of God. The more you study the ministry of Jesus, the better you will recognize the pattern of attack from the religious authorities, and the formula for counterattack demonstrated by Jesus and those who followed Him. We are most vulnerable to attack when we are weakened from difficult circumstances, but we are also vulnerable when we are riding high on victory. When Satan tempted Jesus, He was coming off a 40-day fast. (Matthew 4:1-11) And after He walked on water, deepening the faith of His disciples, Jesus was attacked by the religious leaders. (Matthew 15:1-11).

Sometimes when I think about Jesus' teaching during his earthly ministry, I imagine Him using every means at His disposal to shake people from their lethargy and get them to open their eyes. The Torah (Law) contained 613 written commandments, but it did not always contain instructions on how to carry out those commandments. Eventually, the Talmud (Rabbinic Writings) and the Mishnah (Oral Law) were added to give further instruction and definition to Jewish living.

The religious leaders came to Jesus to point out that His disciples were not compliant with their traditions, and Jesus upped the ante by pointing out how the religious leaders had established and perpetuated a cultural shift from a primary focus on the law and adherence to the law, toward submission to their traditions, which were ostensibly derived from the law. Jesus understood that the law by itself could not produce holiness, but the pharisaic traditions were a step removed from the law, and He was not about to miss the opportunity to point out their hypocrisy.

Let's put this into a modern context using Psalm 150 which is the quintessential psalm of praise. The psalmist says, ***Praise the Lord! Parise God in His sanctuary; praise Him in His mighty expanse. Praise Him for His mighty deeds; praise Him according to His excellent greatness. Praise Him with the trumpet sound; praise Him with harp and lyre. Praise Him with timbrel and dancing; praise Him with stringed instruments and pipe. Praise Him with loud cymbals; praise Him with resounding cymbals. Let everything that has breath praise the Lord. Praise the Lord***.

Psalm 150 is a joyous, celebratory, and jubilant end to one of the most beloved books of the Bible, and although it does tell us to praise God with cymbals, it does not tell us what rhythm to play on the cymbals, it tells us to praise God with the trumpet, but it does not tell us what melody or with what style to play the trumpet. The purpose of this psalm is not to tell us what instruments to use, what melodies to play, what style of music to produce; it simply tells us to praise God and to do so loudly and wholeheartedly. However, in many modern churches and in some denominations, a tradition has emerged that prohibits the use of any instrument other than a piano or an organ, neither of which was even invented when Psalm 150 was written. In several American churches, the race of the predominant group within the congregation will determine the style of music used in worship to the exclusion of all other styles of music. These are examples of the traditions of men circumnavigating and usurping the authority of scripture.

When we understand the scriptures and know their meaning, we can observe multiple examples where people, churches, and even governments claim to honor God with their words, rules, and behaviors, yet what they have actually done is elevate their own traditions above the Word of God. As Jesus ministered, those in His inner circle, those who opposed Him, and the crowds that followed Him, saw Jesus confront ungodly behavior in ways they had never experienced before. We have the ability and the obligation to do as Jesus did, but it starts with making the investment of time to know the scriptures for yourself. The Holy Spirit will always be there to help us, and when someone says something that is not consistent with the will and the Word of God, the Spirit within us tells us to seek the truth and confront the lie with His truth.

Christian Living

In the previous section, we looked at the great commandment found in Matthew 22:37, which is to love God and love others. In Matthew 28:19, we find the great commission, which is a directive from Jesus for us to spread the gospel to the known world. First, Jesus taught His disciples to love God with all their hearts, souls, and minds, and to love others as they love themselves. It was after this great commandment that Jesus gave the great commission to make disciples, and this sequence is important. Jesus didn't say to His disciples, take everything I have taught you and share it with the world. First, Jesus taught them to love God and the world as He loved the world. Fueled by that love, they were commissioned to go throughout the known world telling every group of people that the Savior had come.

Effective missions work and effective ministry are always preceded and fueled by an abiding love for the lost. We discussed love as an action, in contrast to love as a feeling, and only active love can drive a person to abandon their own interests for the sake of someone else. Consider the missionaries to Ecuador who lived and died for the Waodani people. The only thing that explains their sacrifice is love.

The Pharisees asked Jesus, what is the great commandment in the law? In our time, people are asking, " What is Christian living? Whether it is a group of 1st-century Pharisees testing Jesus, or it is a group of 21st-century people who scoff at Christianity, the question is the same, and so is the answer. The Pharisees claimed to know the law, but they tested Jesus to discredit Him. People today will say they know what it means to be a good person without the Bible, so what makes Christian living right? Some will even try to define Christianity in their own terms, but the bottom line is that being a Christian means demonstrating an active love for God and for others. Everything else hangs on the two basic principles of loving God and loving others.

If we are being honest, loving God and loving others can be extremely challenging because loving God means hating the things that God hates, and by nature, we love the things that God hates. Loving others means seeing the image of God in others, and most of us are too preoccupied with seeking our own image in God. We are made in the image of God, but God is not made in our image. However, we can get caught up in assuming that the things we like most about ourselves must be godly attributes. As such, rather than seeing value in other people, at best, we may wait until they look more like us before we are willing to love them.

The connection between the great commandment and the great commission is that loving God and loving others is manifest in spreading the gospel, and this is the very heart of Christian living. If we truly love God, then we will love others, and the most loving thing we can do for others is to share the gospel with them. This is the awesome lesson Jesus taught. Taking this lesson to heart changed the lives and destinies of His disciples and changed the course of human history.

Mark 10:17-31

Disappointment is the result of unmet expectations and embedded in the American Declaration of Independence is an ancient human expectation. *We hold these truths to be self-evident, that all men are created equal, that they are endowed by their creator with certain unalienable rights, that among these are life, liberty, and the pursuit of happiness*. As Americans, we are taught these words from an early age, and by his use of the term, self-evident, there is a sense in which Thomas Jefferson was not relaying a new idea so much as he was speaking of an innate human expectation which we are already aware of.

The Declaration of Independence presumes an understanding that, as human beings, we have a God-given right to life, liberty, and the pursuit of happiness. This assumption is as old as humanity. When Jesus taught that life, liberty, and the pursuit of happiness are not rights given by God, He challenged the foundations of what people were predisposed to believe about the relationship between human beings and their creator. To this day, the very idea that happiness, comfort, and peace are not endowments from our creator is at the root of any secular challenge to the goodness of God, and it forms the basis for great disappointment in God.

In Mark 10:17-22, Jesus was approached by a wealthy man who was ready and willing to follow Him, so long as following Jesus did not encroach on his ongoing pursuit of life, liberty, and happiness. The man approached Jesus with a greeting, "***Good teacher, what shall I do to inherit eternal life?***" Jesus set up His response by alluding to His deity when He pointed out that the man called Him good, but no one is good except God. This statement gave weight and authority to whatever answer Jesus was about to provide, but I want to dwell for a moment on the question the man asked. Materially speaking, the man had everything, but he wanted and expected to receive more. The man wanted to keep what he had while simultaneously acquiring the ultimate prize, which is eternal life. In His response, Jesus told the man that God does not owe anyone an earthly experience of life, liberty, and the pursuit of happiness in addition to eternal life, but that he would have to choose between material things and eternal life.

Jesus did not live in earthly comfort or prosperity, and He promised no such thing to His followers. Throughout His ministry, Jesus continued to describe the full life on earth as a life of service and sacrifice, not a life of pursuing one's own pleasure. Jesus did not promise that we would enjoy pleasant and harmonious family relationships if we follow Him; in fact, He promised the opposite in Matthew 10:34, where He said the cost of following Him would mean tumultuous relationships within the family. Jesus never promised that we would have nice, comfortable homes to live in. He promised the opposite in Matthew 8:20 when He said that following Him could mean times of homelessness. Jesus did not promise that we would have time to bid farewell to those we leave behind to pursue ministry; he promised the opposite in Luke 9:62 when He said anyone holding on to the faith while looking back at what they left behind was not worthy of Him.

In Luke 14:27, Jesus taught that we are to prioritize Him over all other pursuits and all other relationships in our lives. Nearly everything in the teachings of Jesus over the three years He walked with His disciples was a refutation of the idea that God promises life liberty and the pursuit of happiness. Our continued striving for these unalienable rights is what creates disappointment when we come face to face with the God of the Bible.

The wealthy man declined the offer of eternal life and walked away. Although he was probably expecting Jesus to tell him to make a large contribution to the local synagogue or something like that, he was completely unprepared for what Jesus said. The wealthy man was not the only one who was caught off guard by the words of Jesus. The disciples were also amazed at what Jesus said. (Mark 10:24) These men had never considered the incumbrance that holding on to material wealth or personal happiness can cause if one truly desires eternal life. This was likely the first time the disciples had considered that not having material wealth might be advantageous.

Mark 12:41-44

There are many scriptures that give us a composite picture of what Christian living looks like, but the story of the widow's mite, while it takes up only 4 short verses, is broad and pervasive in defining the Christian life. As we consider the story of the widow's mite, we must recognize that giving isn't always material and that sometimes giving needs to be sacrificial, which is characterized by releasing what we have to our own potential detriment. It is also important to recognize that giving, whether material or non-material, will always make the most profound and lasting impact on the life of the giver.

When we read the story of the widow's mite, we ought to notice that the money the widow dropped into the treasury did not put the treasury's fund-raising goals over the top. In fact, the widow's contribution was unnoticed by everyone except the widow and Jesus. Because it was all that she had, you can be certain the widow felt the impact of giving up this small amount of money (Sacrificial giving), even though the money did not make a significant impact on the treasury.

Christian living involves a willingness to give in, to give up, and to give away. Being a Christian means spending a lifetime divesting oneself of any and everything that holds us captive. The connection between Mark 10:17-24 and Mark 12:41-44 is that, whereas the rich man was unwilling to experience the discomfort of poverty, the widow was able and willing to dive deeper into poverty out of an abiding and demonstrable commitment to her faith. There was nothing in her life that restrained her from sacrificial giving. This is what Jesus meant when He said, "***How hard it will be for those who are wealthy to enter the kingdom of God***." (Mark 10:23)

The difficulty for the wealthy person is in separating themselves from the comfort of wealth. Having no wealth, the widow was better equipped to give the little she had. Have you ever felt that way about your faith? Have you ever felt ready and willing to completely divest yourself of everything you cling tightly to just to see the look of joy that surely must have been on the face of Jesus as he taught His disciples what Christian living looks like?

To make this practical, I want to offer some examples of how this might apply in our own lives. Let's consider three things that we are often inclined to cling to, things we are only willing to release when we have them in abundance:

- **Time** – "*When the kids are grown or when I retire, I will spend more time volunteering.*"
- **Treasure** – "*After I have met my household budget, I will give a portion of what remains to the church and charity.*"
- **Tent** – "*If I had adequate space, I would love to open my home up to someone in need.*"

The beauty of what the widow did, and the repugnance of what the rich man failed to do, lies in the widow's willingness to give even when giving was certain to cause her greater suffering. By contrast, the rich man would only suffer financially if he did as Jesus instructed him to do; selling everything he had and gaving it to people like the widow. Therefore, we ought to give of our time when we haven't got a minute to spare. We ought to give of our treasure when there is not enough money in the checking account to pay the bills. We ought to give up the space in our home when it means moving someone into our home while the space is still being occupied by our own family.

Remember, Jesus didn't teach that every rich person should sell what they have and give to the poor. Jesus didn't teach that everyone with a large home must make room for the homeless; He spoke directly to the rich man, just like He sometimes speaks directly to us. When we hear our Lord and

Savior tell us to let go of what we have, we must respond to His call. Jesus didn't tell the widow to give her only a mite; she simply knew it was the right thing to do. There are times in our lives when we simply know the right thing to do is to give, even when it makes no sense to do so, and there are times when we hear Jesus calling us to acts of largess. This is the heart of Christian living. What Jesus taught runs counter to everything we learn from this world and every natural instinct, but there is no joy like giving everything for the sake of our faith in Jesus Christ. If I may put this into a phrase, for the Christian, ***living*** is ***giving***.

Chapter Seven

Preacher

In chapter six, I defined preaching as didactic oration, which moves beyond conventional wisdom and elucidates the Word of God for the purpose of motivating people to think and to live differently. When preaching is done with bold allegiance to the holy scriptures, it can be extremely offensive because it shines the spotlight on the ways we think or live, which are out of alignment with the God of the Bible. We often resist biblical preaching because we naturally love our sin and do not want to be told that we need to correct the way we think or live. This is why people will find any available excuse to dismiss the truth of the Bible and gravitate toward conventional wisdom that does not challenge but rather affirms their lifestyle and thinking. "***For the time will come when they will not endure sound doctrine; but wanting to have their ears tickled, they will accumulate for themselves teachers in accordance with their own desires***" (2 Timothy 4:3)

I came to Christianity like many others. My life was falling apart, and I needed something beyond conventional wisdom to put my life back together. After accepting Christ as my Lord and Savior, I spent a great deal of time listening to Christian radio, and it wasn't the music that got my attention; it was the preaching. I heard one compelling message after another that called me to a higher standard of living, explained the complexities of the human experience, and made sense of the struggles I was facing. The most convincing and compelling messages I heard were based upon the Bible, which gave those messages power and authority.

Later, when I attended seminary, I learned that preaching can be topical, expository, textual, narrative, and biographical. I found myself drawn to expository preaching, which is preaching that explains the meaning of a passage of scripture. By then, I had been reading the Bible, and I was fascinated by what I read, even though I didn't always understand what I read. The preachers I listened to on Christian radio had a way of deconstructing the scriptures and using relevant examples to put Biblical ideas into context for me so that I could make sense of what I was reading. One of my favorite seminary professors, Howard Hendricks, used to say that if you want to do expository preaching, always remember the three pillars of the inductive study process: observation, interpretation, and application. As He spoke to the masses, Jesus demonstrated mastery of these three pillars of preaching.

In this chapter, we will look at Jesus the preacher as we consider what His followers experienced while listening to His sermons, as well as His conversations with and rebukes from the established religious authorities of the day. We will examine how Jesus's exposition of the law and the prophets allowed those who heard Him to see the holy scriptures in a different way, and how the message of Jesus challenges both friend and foe. The homilies of Jesus, as well as the personal interactions between Jesus and His disciples, shook people from their lethargy and charted a course from ignorance and complacency to good works and self-sacrifice. As we examine His sermons and the audacious confrontations Jesus had, we will try to imagine what those who were in His presence felt as He proclaimed the Word of God.

Although Jesus preached many sermons, two of His orations, the Sermon on the Mount and the Mount of Olives discourse, stand out among the others. We will look at both sermons and some of His shorter messages as we seek to understand how Jesus the preacher impacted those in His inner circle as well as the multitudes He ministered to.

The Sermon On The Mount

In the year 382, Pope Damasus commissioned Jerome, a Latin Scholar, to translate the gospels into Latin, but it was over 1,200 years later in 1611 that King James had the Bible translated into English. We refer to the section of the Sermon on the Mount in Matthew 5:3-11 as the beatitudes, which comes from the Latin word beatus, meaning blessed or happy. Over the centuries, the term beatitudes became the accepted title for this section of Matthew's gospel. In the beatitudes, Jesus ascribed blessedness to nine states of being which no one then or now would have associated with happiness. These nine blessings are ascribed to those who:

1. Are Poor in spirit
2. Mourn
3. Are gentle
4. Hunger and thirst for righteousness
5. Are merciful
6. Are pure in heart
7. Are peacemakers
8. Have been persecuted for the sake of righteousness
9. Are insulted and falsely accused

When I was engaged in business, I learned that one of the key differences between an entrepreneur and someone who is not an entrepreneur is that the entrepreneur is not easily deterred by the prospect of risk. It is human nature to be uncomfortable exchanging that which is right in front of us, for that which we cannot yet see. We have heard the expression, "A bird in the hand is worth two in the bush", but in the beatitudes, Jesus is saying that to obtain the two birds in a bush, you will need to invest the one in your hand. This is problematic because it is most common for people to look at what they have now and guard it zealously for fear of losing everything precious to them.

The beatitudes were not Jesus giving a formula for happiness or success; He was pointing out that, contrary to conventional wisdom, those whose dispositions and afflictions put them at a disadvantage ***now*** will have a reward ***later***. The reason we tend to hold on to everything we can see now is that we fear this is as good as things will ever be. Jesus is saying that if you are willing to risk poverty in spirit now, you will receive wealth in heaven. If you are willing to risk experiencing pain and mourning now, hang in there; you will be comforted later. If you can forsake the immediate advantage of aggression now, you will inherit the earth later. If what you truly hunger for is righteousness now, in the future you will be satisfied. All of this is about delayed gratification, which is something we are often very uncomfortable with because it is risky, and as human beings, we are often risk averse.

The beatitudes end in Matthew 5:11, but the explanation Jesus gives for all that He said in verses 3-11 continues. In verse 12, Jesus encourages His followers to rejoice despite their current circumstances because they will be richly rewarded in heaven. Starting in Matthew 5:13 through verse 20, Jesus continues to explain that His followers are to be and to think differently from the rest of the world. Jesus encouraged His followers to live today with a focus on the unseen tomorrow. The remainder of the Sermon on the

Mount takes on a range of subjects, including divorce, the Christian attitude toward giving, fasting, judging, treating others as we want to be treated, and how to recognize false prophets when they come.

The Sermon on the Mount is extremely practical, but I don't want you to miss its expository elements. Jesus offers new meaning to numerous Old Testament scriptures from Deuteronomy, Proverbs, Exodus, 2 Samuel, Leviticus, Psalms, Isaiah, Jeremiah, and even Ruth. These scriptures would have been familiar to those listening to Him, but as Jesus preaches, He creates a deeper understanding of these scriptures, which, for some, had been difficult to apply to their own lives.

Whereas in His shorter sermons, where His messages were brief, the Sermon on the Mount covered a vast amount of material and unlocked meaning for His followers that was previously unknown to them. This sermon was life-altering because it not only unveiled so much about the will of God, but it also set the standard for our calling in Christ.

The Mount Olivet Discourse

The Mount Olivet Discourse began with Jesus proclaiming the future destruction of the temple and His disciples asking when it would occur. The Mount Olivet Discourse is future-oriented, but rather than providing His disciples with the exact time when events would unfold, Jesus focused their thoughts and attitudes on the present so they could be prepared for future events. Whereas Jesus directly addressed our thoughts, actions, and motives in the Sermon on the Mount, in the Mount Olivet discourse, Jesus described the end of days so that we would spend the time we have now in preparation for what is to come. Jesus did not want His disciples to focus on when the end would come; He wanted them to know that while the end would be a time of great tribulation, these events need not catch them off guard.

All the examples Jesus gave in the Mount Olivet Discourse had common elements. The examples Jesus provided described events that were:

- Predictable
    - While we do not know the day or time the end will come, we can know for certain that the end will come.
- Inevitable
    - While we can prepare ourselves for what is to come, we cannot avoid these things. End-time events are predestined, and there is nothing we can do to avoid the future collapse of this system.

There is much written in the Bible about the end times, but nothing in the Mount Olivet discourse or anywhere else in the Bible offers a plan to delay, alter, or avoid end-time events. God delays end-time events for us so that we have an opportunity to change our hearts and to warn others. While we cannot avoid the end-time events themselves, we can avoid the eternal consequences of damnation. In the Mount Olivet Discourse, Jesus gives us guidance on how to prepare ourselves and others for the last days.

The Power Of Good Storytelling

Soon after I returned home from seminary, I became part of the preaching team at a local church. The senior pastor would determine the theme for each Wednesday and Sunday message, and as the newest member of the team, I was required to submit the outline for my message to my supervisor in advance. The feedback I received was often that rather than focusing on the biblical text, I needed to tell more personal stories, but I wanted to do exegetical preaching wherein I stuck to the biblical text and explained each verse of scripture. I reasoned that there was little of value in my personal stories, but that the Word of God is rich with life-changing messages that the congregation needed to hear.

During His discourses, Jesus told stories about His life and about things that were soon to come, which were and are still worth hearing and understanding. My personal anecdotes do not have the power to set anyone on the path toward righteousness, but the Word of God has the power to lead people into the presence of God. Therefore, it seems to me that while personal stories can help to connect people to biblical messages, the primary focus needs to be on God's Word.

Storytelling has always been an integral part of any human society. Great storytellers captivate their audiences with tales of heroes and villains, which give us a sense of hope and adventure. Personally, I have always loved books and movies about superheroes who vanquish evil foes and defend the powerless. The unpredictability and perilous nature of life cause us to create and to enjoy stories of superheroes verses maniacal villains, and if you look for it, you will find that writers of superhero fantasy sometimes borrow from biblical characters and themes.

My favorite superhero has always been Superman. In the 1978 Superman film starring Christopher Reeve, Superman's father, Jor-el, played by Marlon Brando, delivered an interesting monologue. In this monologue, Jor-el said to his son, "Live *among the humans, they can be a great people if they wish to be, but they only lack the light to show them the way. For this reason, above all, their capacity for good, I have sent them you, my only son.*" Superman, whose given name is Kal-el, was a survivor of the doomed planet Krypton, which was destroyed because the Kryptonians ignored warnings from Jor-el, much like humans ignored warnings by Noah, who survived a planet-wide deluge. It is also interesting that Jor-el and Kal- el, are names derived from the ancient Hebrew word El, meaning God. In this case, the film writers may have taken the messianic doctrine of Jesus as Son of God and infused it with the humanist doctrine of the goodness of humanity.

In 2012, Marvel released the first Avengers movie, and I was hooked. Over the next seven years, three additional Avengers movies were released in addition to a slew of other Marvel feature films and TV shows based on Avengers characters. The villain of the second and third Avengers movies, "Infinity War" and "End Game," was a malevolent character named Thanos, whose life's work was to reduce the population of the entire universe by half. Thanos would often repeat the phrase, "*I am inevitable*". Thanos had a fore runner of sorts named Ebony Maw, who proclaimed to Thanos's victims how blessed they were to be sacrificed for the grand agenda of Thanos. This can be seen as a subtle way of assigning malevolent intent to John the Baptist, who proclaimed the coming of the Lord, and Jesus, our Savior.

After acquiring all of the infinity stones, Thanos was able to snap his fingers and immediately accomplish his objective, instantly reducing the population of the universe by half, which looks suspiciously like the rapture described in the New Testament. Once Thanos accomplished his goal, he retired to "The Garden," where he was hunted down and killed by the Avengers. Of course, I cannot say for certain that the writers of either DC or Marvel Comics stole their ideas from the Bible, but these thematic concepts in hero lore can make it difficult for people who do not understand or embrace the Christian faith to understand Christian doctrine or theology.

I mention all of this because, although I enjoy the art and good storytelling, it is important that I effectively discern between fantasy and reality and that I am always aware of how the enemy uses confusion and distortion of biblical truth to create a wide range of attitudes from ignorance, to apathy, to animus, in an effort to throw humanity off track. Jesus, not Superman, nor Thor, was sent down from heaven to save us from eternal destruction. Rather than being irritated or feeling indignant when we recognize biblical influence on secular art, I think there is cause for hope because this shows us that the eschatology Jesus spoke of thousands of years ago, and the messianic hope, are still strong in the human heart, and there is an apparent longing for what Jesus alone can provide.

As Jesus gave His Mount Olivet discourse, His disciples heard about the horrors that were to come, but they also heard from the Savior who would redeem them from this calamity. Human beings have always lived with fear of future events, and as our folklore reveals, we have always hoped for someone who is more powerful than the trials that are coming. We know that men in capes are not real, but Jesus is real, and His disciples were comforted during the Mount Olivet discourse by the knowledge that they were in the presence of the Savior of humankind. They were comforted by the knowledge that the message He preached contained life-transforming truth. This is the essence of effective, biblical preaching; it has the capacity to change lives.

Childlike Faith

There is no doubt that Jesus loves children. We know this because children are people, and Jesus loves people. However, based upon my reading of the scriptures, it seems to me that what Jesus loved about children is their optimism, faith, openness, humility, and their inquisitive nature. Children want to learn and grow, but as we approach adulthood, we become haughty, defensive, closed, and skeptical. In Matthew 18:1-11, the disciples came to Jesus and asked, "***Who then is greatest in the kingdom of heaven?***" The disciples were not asking Jesus to name a specific person; they were asking about a *type* of person who would have the most desirable attributes in the kingdom of heaven. They wanted to know what character qualities they should develop so that they would be acceptable in heaven. In response, Jesus said, "***Unless you are converted and become like children, you will not enter the kingdom of heaven.***" This statement has often been misunderstood as Jesus saying that children will be given preferential treatment over adults, and that is not what Jesus was saying. Jesus was using the example of children to make the point that we need to retain our childlike qualities of trust, openness, humility, and tender-heartedness.

Anyone who has ever been a parent can think of multiple examples of when their children demonstrated total faith and dependence upon them, and every time I think about that state of complete trust between child and parent, an example comes to mind. When my youngest daughter was about three years old, she would listen for the sound of the garage door opening and my car coming into the garage. As I walked from the garage into the house, I would find her standing on the third step from the bottom with her eyes closed and her arms spread wide. When she heard the door which led from the garage into the house open, she would fall forward into my arms, trusting that I would catch her.

Sometimes, when I was carrying packages and not thinking about her little ritual, I had to drop everything in my arms so that I could catch her before she did a face plant onto the floor. I thought about that example when she was selling her first car, and she asked me to be with her during the sale. The buyer asked how much she would accept for the car, and she turned to me and said, "*I fully trust my father to negotiate on my behalf.*" Despite the fact that she was 26 years old at the time, she had not lost her childlike trust in me. This is an example of what Jesus is looking for in His followers.

For some of us, as brand-new Christians, we were full of hope, trust, and an indomitable spirit, and that was me when I first gave my life to Christ. I was bold, intrepid, and loud about my faith. Over the years, I have retained my trust in Jesus, but hopefully I am less obnoxious and more mature in the way I live out my faith. Yet, as a man of faith, I am still very much like my three-year-old daughter, eyes closed, arms wide open, falling into the embrace of Jesus. This is what Jesus meant when He spoke to His disciples while calling the children to come to Him.

These children were models of Christian faith and humility. This message had a profound effect on His disciples, and from that message, they received an important answer to their initial question, "***Who then is greatest in the kingdom of heaven?***" Jesus provided them with an example of how to grow in knowledge and strength, while remaining simple and faith-filled like a child. By contrast, Jesus also warned us that anyone who works to harden the heart of a tender-hearted, childlike Christian would suffer the wrath of judgment.

Love That Confronts And Corrects

The first time I heard a preacher say that Jesus was offensive, I thought I had heard him incorrectly, but I learned over the years that Jesus was and continues to be offensive. He was offensive to the religious authorities of the first century, and He is offensive to those today who want a watered-down, inclusive gospel that allows everyone to feel good about themselves as they are. I will close this chapter by reviewing a message from Jesus spoken in Luke 11:37-53, but before we get to that scripture, I want to share a quote from C.S. Lewis, who wrote, "*My prayer is that when I die, all of hell rejoices that I am out of the fight.*" What an incredible epitaph! We are all called to be examples of the love of Jesus, but we are also called to be Satan's nemesis and to rebuke him as Jesus did. Because the world system produces emissaries of evil, we as Christians become offensive to those who want to perpetuate the current world system.

When one of the Pharisees invited Jesus to have lunch at his home, he had no idea that Jesus was not interested in being a good and polite guest who just went along with social norms. Jesus was interested in speaking the truth regardless of who might be offended by what He had to say. We should all have that level of audacity!

The imagery of Luke 11:37-53 is vivid; Jesus had just spoken to a large crowd, condemning a generation of people who had everything they needed for repentance, yet they refused to do so. To make His point, Jesus used examples such as that of the Queen of Sheba, who came to visit King Solomon and was moved by the multiple blessings God had given him. Jesus also reminded the crowd of the Ninevites and how God used Jonah to warn them that they must repent of their evil or face eternal consequences. The Pharisees heard all of this and knew Jesus was alluding to their evil hearts. The Pharisees had invited Jesus to lunch, thinking they would put Him in an awkward social situation, but the plan backfired on them miserably. During the meal, the Pharisee who hosted the meal took the opportunity to criticize Jesus and His disciples for not observing their ceremonial hand-washing practices. In a stinging rebuke, Jesus replied with one offensive indictment after another. Jesus accused the Pharisees of:

- **False piety** – Presenting themselves as clean, pious, and knowledgeable, on the outside, while being filthy and full of malice on the inside
- **False worship** – Offering tithes to God for appearances, while denying justice to the people of God
- **False Identity** – Claiming to hold a lofty position within society, while in reality, they were like unmarked tombs that people walked over as if they were not even there

After one intrepid lawyer weighed in to say his feelings were hurt by Jesus's comments, Jesus turned His attention to the lawyers, indicting them of:

- **Hypocrisy** – They placed burdens on men that they would not bear themselves
- **Murder** – While previous generations killed the prophets, this generation approved their deaths by continuing to disregard their counsel
- **Suppression** – They withheld ancient teaching given to Israel by God for their edification

According to the Pew Research Center's 2023-24 Religious Landscape Study (RLS), 62% of US adults describe themselves as Christians. My understanding of Christianity as I grew up was ambiguous at best, but I understood that being a Christian meant believing in Jesus and doing good. Although as a young adult I would have described myself as a Christian, I didn't know much about Jesus, I just thought He was a nice, gentle, non-confrontational man who lived a long time ago.

I think most people are shocked to see the side of Jesus who got angry and confronted hypocrisy and evil head on. We tend to see Jesus as a historical figure, and to better understand historical figures we polarize them into categories that make sense to us. As such, it may not occur to us that being like Jesus might require being assertively confrontational during family or social gatherings when people present an ungodly or even heretical view of Christianity.

It is important to respect the right of others to express their opinions, and in most instances, there is no need for us to correct people who are set in their beliefs, but there does come a time when we need to be assertively confrontational about truth. For example, when someone misquotes scripture, it is important to direct them to the text and assertively point out what the scripture actually says. Or, if someone says that Jesus was married and had children, we ought to challenge them and ask them to show us where they find that in the Bible. Conversations like this will always feel awkward because we live in a day and time where people expect Christians to simply accept whatever version of Christianity is trending at the time. The Apostle Paul forewarned us about this in 2 Timothy 4:3 saying, "***For the***

time will come when they will not endure sound doctrine; but wanting to have their ears tickled, they will accumulate for themselves teachers in accordance to their own desires."

When Jesus stood up in the Pharisee's own home and corrected him with authority, He was giving His disciples an example of what it looks like to love someone enough to correct them. Although Jesus was firm, perhaps even offensive, He was not malicious. So much is said and written about love, and precious little of it is true. When you love someone, you are morally obligated to let them know when they are suffering from a life-threatening condition. The least loving thing one can do is to pretend all is well when all is not well.

I will close with this example. In 1837 Hans Christian Anderson published the children's story, "The Emperor's New Clothes". Most of us are familiar with the story which depicts a vein, gullible, emperor who was tricked into parading through his kingdom naked while believing he was dressed in the finest apparel. Although many of the emperor's subjects paid homage as he publicly humiliated himself, none of them other than a small child demonstrated enough courage or curiosity to speak the truth and blurt out that the emperor wore no clothes at all. Even though in the story, the pompous Emperor continued his parade out of foolish pride, the child spoke the truth where no one else would. In a sense, Jesus pointed out that the Pharisee's doctrine was naked and lacking any effective substance. During the encounter between Jesus, the Pharisees, and the Lawyers, Jesus taught His disciples the value and importance of honestly confronting falsehood with truth and integrity.

Chapter Eight

Pastor

Pastors are shepherds, but only to the extent that their congregations are like sheep. Within Christianity, the term pastor is used as a leadership title, and shepherding is what the pastor is expected to do. There are a few other terms used for church leadership, including priest, reverend, minister, and father, but the one we are going to focus on is pastor, and I think we will find that there is much more to pastoral care than just a title.

Jesus is the consummate shepherd. (John 10:11) He is the one who leads and who lays down His life for the flock; and we expect pastors to demonstrate those shepherd-like qualities as they serve their congregations. In this chapter, we will look at how the followers of Jesus witnessed and experienced His pastoral care. We want to know what it was like to be part of Jesus's flock, and in what ways His followers felt protected, provided for, and special; we want to discover how Jesus demonstrated compassion for His flock. We know there were other rabbis during Jesus's time on earth, so we want to understand what made being a part of Jesus's flock different than others who were making a name for themselves during this time, and why the followers of Jesus were so impressed with Him as their pastor.

King David and the son of God

Jesus engaged in a fascinating theological discussion with the Pharisees in Matthew 22:41-45 when He asked them what they thought about the Christ and whose son He was. The Pharisees' said Christ is the son of David. Jesus responded by asking them, "***If the Christ is the son of David,***

how does David in the Spirit call Him Lord, saying, The Lord said to my Lord sit at My right Hand, until I put Your enemies beneath Your feet?" Quoting Psalm 110, Jesus continued, "***If David then calls Him Lord, how is He his son?***"

One of the most memorable and comforting chapters in the Bible is Psalm 23, where King David describes his relationship with the Lord, and it was centuries later that Christians adopted the doctrine of trinitarianism. While the early church fathers did not invent the concept of a triune God, they codified these already held beliefs based upon a comprehensive understanding of the scriptures, put together a systematic theology, and organized our doctrines. David understood that one facet of his relationship with God was that He led, protected, and guided him throughout his life.

Although David would not have been aware of Jesus by name, he did experience the fullness of the Godhead as expressed in the Father, the Son, and the Holy Spirit. As he wrote Psalm 23, the image of a shepherd was familiar and accessible to David because of the era in which he lived. In addition, David's first career was as a shepherd. David used this image of the divine shepherd as he described his relationship with God the Son.

The powerful, visceral emotions evoked by Psalm 23 reach far beyond the ancient Near East context in which David lived and wrote the psalm. People within and outside the Judeo-Christian faith find it easy to relate to these images of comfort and care. I want us to briefly touch on this psalm as we connect its content with our expectation of Jesus and as we look to these qualities of pastoral care contemporarily. Psalm 23 offers 6 distinct pastoral attributes of Jesus:

1. **Providence** – The Lord is my shepherd; I shall not want. (12:1) Like a shepherd providing for his sheep, Jesus provides for all of our needs so that we want for nothing
2. **Peace** – He makes me lie down in green pastures; He leads me beside quiet waters. (12:2) Sheep are naturally docile creatures that are easily scared. Rushing water scares sheep and makes them nervous. The good shepherd leads his sheep by still waters, which provides an atmosphere of calm and peace.
3. **Proprietorship** – He restores my soul; He guides me in the paths of righteousness ***for His name's sake***. (12:3) Notice that restoration of the soul and guiding in the path of righteousness are done for the sake, reputation, and glory of the Lord.
4. **Protection** – Even though I walk through the valley of the shadow of death, I fear no evil, for You are with me; Your rod and Your staff, they comfort me. (23:4) The shepherd's rod and staff were weapons used to fight off predators and defend the flock. The valley of the shadow of death is an image of life's many perils and our own fragility. Knowing that our shepherd is armed and ready to defend us does not remove the peril or negate our fragility, but it does remind us that we are under divine protection.
5. **Potency** – You prepare a table before me in the presence of my enemies; You have anointed my head with oil; My cup overflows. (23:5) Reclining, relaxing, and eating, in the presence of one's enemies, is an outward expression of a calm, fearless, inner strength and power. The image of power is further expressed in that oil was poured over the head

of kings to confirm their reign. The fact that David described his cup as overflowing with oil indicates that the oil for anointing will never run out; it is eternal

6. **Presence** – Surely goodness and lovingkindness will follow me all the days of my life, and I will dwell in the house of the Lord forever. (23:6) It is interesting how David conflates the idea of kinetic and akinetic energy in this verse. Being followed by lovingkindness indicates kinesis, while dwelling in the house of the Lord is a picture of akinesis or remaining in one place. Both of these concepts create an image of the Lord's abiding presence. Whether we are at home or moving about, the Lord is eternally present.

The Good Shepherd

I once saw a video where test subjects stood before flocks of sheep and tried to get the sheep to follow them, but the sheep ignored the test subjects. Then, when the real shepherd called the flock, they responded by running to him. Sheep know their master's voice, and they respond. While speaking to a crowd after restoring sight to a blind man, Jesus referred to Himself as the Good Shepherd. (John 10:11) The Pharisees responded to Jesus healing the blind man by putting the man out of the synagogue because he had been healed on the sabbath, and the man would not renounce Jesus as a sinner for breaking the sabbath laws. The point Jesus was making when He referred to Himself as the good shepherd is that people are capable of differentiating between good and evil, and that those who were of His flock would know His voice, and they would know the difference between truth and false doctrine.

During His teaching in John 10:1-18, Jesus also described Himself as the door to the sheepfold. He is the voice that true believers respond to and that all those who came before Him, trying to pull sheep from the fold, claiming to be sent from the Father, were impostors who have only come to steal, kill, and destroy. In this, Jesus was keeping with His metaphor of the relationship between the shepherd and the sheep. This metaphor of a shepherd with his sheep is extremely relevant for today because any pastor or preacher with his or her own agenda speaks for themselves, and they do so for self-gain. Imposters come into the flock to:

- **Steal** – Thieves siphon off gullible congregants who are not fully committed to or interested in the truth
- **Kill** – When people follow false doctrine, they perish (Spiritual Death), and this is what the devil wants
- **Destroy** – As individuals and groups of people fall away after false doctrine, it destroys the sheepfold (The Church)

The compassion of Christ

As Jesus went about teaching, preaching, healing, and casting out demons, the crowd size grew with His fame, and as He ministered, he entered into the pain and suffering of those to whom He ministered.

The most enigmatic aspect of the crucifixion is not the passion of Christ, but the compassion of Christ. Passion is the capacity to experience emotion and to be motivated by it; compassion is the capacity to connect oneself with the plight of others. Jesus experienced passion during His cruel interrogation, trial, and crucifixion, but it was compassion that brought Him to the cross.

It would be easy to understand God holding a distant yet potent love for His creation, but it is nearly impossible to comprehend Jesus, the Son of God, the third member of the trinity, having love and compassion for humanity after living among us for thirty-three years and experiencing our worst as He painfully laid down His life for us. Scripture tells us that seeing the people, Jesus felt compassion for them. (Matthew 9:35-36). Jesus did not just teach and preach; He connected, and He was the ultimate compassionate pastor. Consider, for a moment, the following human examples of uncharacteristic compassion:

- An eighteenth-century Black American slave, who had been beaten with a whip his entire life. He watched his children beaten and kicked, and he witnessed his wife beaten and raped. This slave runs into a burning house and carries out the master who was the source of his deepest pain and humiliation all the days of his life.
- A woman who was abused physically and emotionally runs to the neighbor's house to summon help for her dying husband, the man responsible for making her life miserable since the day she married him.
- A child who never received love, mercy, encouragement, or joy; a child who was never been read to, or given a toy on Christmas, or a hug from a parent. This unloved child then spoons medicine into the mouth of their abusive mother or bandages the wounds on the feet of the father who kicked him daily just for being born.

All of these examples fall far short of describing the compassion of Jesus as He ministered here on earth after voluntarily leaving His heavenly domain to save humanity. This capacity to enter into our pain even after we have denied Him, coupled with the desire to see us made whole and brought into relationship with the God of the universe, is what the disciples witnessed on full display as they walked with Jesus. However, the compassion Jesus felt was not exclusively for His disciples, it was for all humanity, and it is this compassion for others that caused the explosive growth of His ministry both before and after His crucifixion.

Jesus gave us the Great Commission, which compels us to make disciples of all nations, but when church growth is an end in itself, the results can be unfortunate. If compassion for the lost is absent from evangelism, all we do is move Christians from one church to another, but the kingdom as a whole does not necessarily grow. When this occurs, we only rearrange the seats in the kingdom as opposed to expanding it.

We live in a world that needs and wants what Jesus has to offer, and that has always been the case, but the world sees through condescension disguised as compassion. People are drawn to outward-focused ministries where they know someone cares about the plight of others. Pastors and congregants who have true compassion for unsaved, unloved people will grow the church. This was the formula used by Jesus. He had compassion for the lost, and that compassion became the driving force behind church growth.

Biblical examples of pastoral shepherding

- 1 Peter 5:2-4
- 2 Samuel 78:72
- Psalm 78:52
- Ezekiel 34

- Psalm 100:3
- John 21

Trojan Horse of the Christian Church

A major concern of Jesus and any pastor today is ensuring the impregnability of the church. The church ought to exist as a fortress surrounding the flock, isolating its members from the enemy's attacks. The church should have doors that allow the lost to enter and join the flock, but it should also have high and unscalable walls that keep predators out. Divorce functions like a Trojan horse within Christianity, and it is disguised as a gift or as something good and useful. We who are within the church open the gates and willingly allow divorce inside. Once inside, it consumes families from within and weakens the entire church.

Perhaps the most definitive statement in the Bible on divorce can be found in Malachi 2:16, where the prophet says, "***For I hate divorce, says the Lord, the God of Israel, and him who covers his garment with wrong, says the Lord of hosts. So, take heed to your spirit, that you do not deal treacherously.***" However, the ESV renders Malachi 2:16 as, "***For the man who does not love his wife but divorces her, says the Lord, the God of Israel, covers his garment with violence, says the Lord of hosts. So, guard yourselves in your spirit and do not be faithless"***. While the ESV does not include the phrase, "***I hate divorce, says the Lord***", everything written about marriage in God's word, including the ESV, makes His love for marriage, and His hatred for anything that causes the dissolution of marriage, clear. Therefore, regardless of which version of Malachi 2:16 you read, God's feelings about marriage and divorce throughout scripture are unambiguous.

Despite this clear and unambiguous statement of God, from the time Moses brought the 10 commandments down from Mount Sinai, the people of God continue to accept and even court divorce as something good, useful, and acceptable to God. The fact is that whereas marriage serves the purpose and plan of God, divorce serves the purpose and plan of human beings. Put another way, marriage serves the Spirit, and divorce serves the flesh.

Making the argument that divorce is acceptable in some circumstances because some versions of the Bible do not contain the phrase, ***God hates divorce***, is like making the case that because there are no passages in the Bible where God says He hates physical, psychological, or sexual abuse, means that in some cases these things are acceptable or necessary. When we justify our ungodly behavior by pointing out that the Bible does not give examples of where God specifically says he hates something, we ignore the truth that the Bible reveals the character of God, and it was never intended to be a comprehensive book of things we must or must not do. The Bible was written to bring us into a closer and deeper relationship with our Creator by describing His character and compelling us to conform to His image.

God gave us marriage because He understands its intrinsic value to individuals, couples, families, and communities. The devil also understands the value of marriage, which is why it has been under attack since the very beginning. Immediately after the original sin, we see Adam and Eve blaming one another rather than walking in harmony as they had been. Moses gave Israel God's ten commandments, and the seventh of these commandments is, "***You shall not commit adultery***." (Exodus 20:14) Like a spiritual palindrome, adultery leads to divorce, and divorce leads to adultery.

Adultery occurs when someone who is married goes outside the marriage for physical and emotional intimacy, which leaves the marriage vulnerable to divorce. When a married couple separates or becomes legally divorced, in the eyes of God, they are still married. In this circumstance, both parties are likely to become physically and emotionally intimate with someone other than their spouse. (Luke 16:18) Jesus makes it clear that when a person who has been joined in marriage by God divorces that person and marries someone else, it is tantamount to adultery. In fact, Jesus taught that adultery starts when a married person simply looks at someone with the thought of sexual intimacy. (Matthew 5:27-28, 19:4-9) Such are the depths of Jesus's convictions about marriage and His disdain for divorce.

As Jesus taught in the region of Judea, the Pharisees attacked the institution of marriage and defended what had become a culture of divorce by asking Jesus whether it was lawful for a man to divorce a wife. Jesus responded by going back to Genesis when God gave us the gift of marriage. (Mark 10:1-11) Rather than anchoring their teaching on the Word of God, the Pharisees followed one of two extreme rabbinic positions on divorce: Shammai or Hillel. Even today, there are intelligent and well-respected members of the Christian community who teach polarized views on the subject. Some teach that there is no Biblical exception for divorce, and others teach that there are multiple circumstances wherein divorce is Biblically acceptable. There is a wealth of good information on the two rabbinic positions of Hillel and Shammai, but we will not get into those positions here.

Suffices to say that the two positions represented polarized views on divorce, but Jesus based His teachings on scripture.

Keep in mind that the thief comes to steal, and kill, and destroy; (John 10:10) and divorce does all three. The pastoral position of Jesus on divorce was and is, don't do it, because divorce **steals** joy, **kills** families, and **destroys** congregations, communities, and society. Not much has changed since the 1st century in attitudes and teaching on divorce. As previously mentioned, there are prominent teachers who preach that there are Biblical grounds for divorce, while other teachers claim there are no Biblical grounds for divorce. However, the effects of divorce are an inescapable reality for families inside the church as well as those outside the church. Jesus understood that divorce and multiple marriages were a clear and present danger for families, and the Bible has a great deal to say about marriage beginning in Genesis and continuing through the New Testament. The Bible speaks about the union of man and woman through the context of:

- **Marriage**
    - Genesis 2:18-25
    - Hosea 1-3
    - Ecclesiastes 4:9-11
    - Song of Solomon
    - Proverbs 18:22
    - Matthew 19:4-6
    - 1 Corinthians 7:1-16
    - Ephesians 5:22-33
    - Colossians 3:18-19
    - Hebrews 13:4
    - 1 Peter 3:1-9

- **Intimacy**
  - Genesis 2:25
  - 1 Corinthians 7:1-5
  - Song of Solomon
- **Procreation**
  - Genesis 1:28
  - Genesis 4:1-2
  - Psalm 127:3-5
- **Child Rearing**
  - Proverbs 13:24
  - Proverbs 22:6
  - Hebrews 12:7-11
- **Fidelity**
  - Exodus 20:14
- **Marital Separation**
  - 1 Corinthians 7:5

Some of the adverse effects of divorce include, but are not limited to:

- **Finances**
  - All members of the family suffer financially from divorce because it requires families to do twice as much with the same finite resources. It becomes more difficult to find adequate housing, both parents are forced to generate income outside the home, and there are fewer financial resources available for recreation.
- **Child rearing**
  - Coparenting may become necessary, but it is not ideal for raising children. Even under the best of circumstances, it is difficult for children to navigate both parents' parenting

styles and adapt to two sets of rules in two different homes.

- **<u>Parental promiscuity</u>**
  - Divorce often leads to remarriage, or both parents establish new relationships with people other than their original spouse. Also, meeting new people and creating dating relationships makes parents vulnerable to promiscuity.
- **<u>Child promiscuity</u>**
  - As children see their parents experimenting with sex outside of marriage, they begin to question the sanctity and the promise of marital exclusivity and fidelity.
- **<u>Diminished capacity to supervise children</u>**
  - As the relationship between parents breaks down, adequately supervising children becomes more of a challenge.

Broken families go into survival mode and therefore have a diminished capacity for a God-centered lifestyle. Therefore, when the Pharisees approached Jesus about divorce, He took them right back to God's original intent for marriage, that a man and a woman would become one flesh and that no one should separate what God has put together. (Matthew 19:5-6) As the ultimate pastor, Jesus fiercely defended the sanctity of marriage because of the protection marriage offers to families, congregations, communities, and the world.

Chapter Nine

Activist

I grew up and came of age during the turbulent 60s. As a child, my world was a collage of causes, and if there was one prevalent, unifying theme, it was the necessity and urgency of imminent and long overdue change. I saw the LA riots on television, I saw the Viet Nam war protests, student resistance that took place at schools like UC Berkeley, and I understood that our government was broken and in need of reform. I remember the day I learned that Martin Luther King had been assassinated, and how my mother wept. I also remember the protests that followed King's death. Even before I heard anyone calling that era the turbulent 60s, I knew I was living in turbulent times.

As a new Christian in 1998, I pondered the connection between Dr. Martin Luther King, a Southern Baptist preacher, and the mechanisms of social activism. I never doubted that Dr. King's work was important, nor did I ever question the positive impact his non-violent movement had on our nation, but I wondered what social activism had to do with our primary mandate as Christians, which I believed and continue to believe is the call to evangelism. Perhaps more importantly, I wondered where social activism fit in with the agenda of Jesus. In this chapter, we will explore:

- The ways and the circumstances in which followers of Jesus witnessed Him working to bring about changes in the social order of the 1st-century Near East.
- How Jesus convicted people of ignoring the poor while they exalted the rich and powerful.

- What Jesus said and did to engage people in creating a paradigm shift.
- Whether the words and actions of Jesus were directed more toward the government of Rome, the Sanhedrin, or the common people.

The more I discuss Christianity broadly, or Jesus specifically, I realize that there is a considerable amount of disagreement about who Jesus was as a historical figure and His relevance today. There are a few questions at the epicenter of these disagreements that we ought to consider as we seek to truly understand Jesus, such as:

- Why did Jesus feed 5,000 people and then 4,000 people?
- Why did Jesus turn water into wine?
- Why did Jesus heal the sick and give sight to the blind?

Viewing these historical events through the lens of pragmatism or liberalism, we might conclude that if Jesus fed 5,000 people, He did so because they were hungry and He wanted to meet their immediate need for food. We might also conclude that if Jesus turned water into wine, He did so because the wine had run out and He wanted to do something practical for the bride and groom. Further, we might conclude that Jesus healed the sick and gave sight to the blind because blind people need to see, and sick people need to get well.

The humanist worldview puts the human at the center of everything, including religion, because the humanist worldview says that if God exists, He exists for the well-being of humanity. A Biblical, theocentric worldview informs us that human beings exist to glorify God, and that Jesus did the things He did in pursuit of that end.

The theocentric worldview does not suggest that Jesus is indifferent to the needs of humanity. Hunger, sickness, and scarcity of resources are all the result of a fallen world plagued by sin. However, the ministry of Jesus is not to relieve the effects of sin, but to lift humanity above sin. Consider these analogies derived from the function of firefighters and police officers.

The fire department in your community has two important functions: one function is firefighting, and the other function is fire prevention. Your local police department has two important functions: one function is crime fighting, and the other is crime prevention. A firefighter who is committed to keeping the community safe realizes he/she can save more lives by teaching residents how to avoid fire hazards than by simply responding to every fire that occurs. By the same token, a police department can be far more effective at protecting the community through teaching residents how to avoid becoming victims of crime than by simply responding to every 911 call.

A firefighter does not assume that he/she can eliminate the destructive power of fire, he/she extends their arm of protection by teaching fire prevention. A police officer knows that he/she cannot eliminate crime, so he/she extends their arm of protection by teaching crime prevention. Jesus did not come to eliminate the effects and consequences of sin, but He extends His arm of protection by offering eternal salvation and by teaching us how to live now without succumbing to the ravages of sin.

Jesus was not unaware of or indifferent to the suffering of humanity; His heart for the suffering of people led Him to chart out a path toward victory by teaching us to focus on God and His commandments. As such, the effectiveness of any ministry is to some degree dependent upon its ability to teach people submission to the great commandment, which is to love God, and then to love other people. When we learn to love God and to glorify Him, we are far less inclined to harm, dismiss, abuse, neglect, or mistreat other people, but we first need to be taught to love and be in awe of our God.

Activism is most often a means of altering the social order so that the scales are tipped in favor of an oppressed or underrepresented group of people. The underlying assumption that motivates this sort of activism is that every human being deserves to be treated with dignity, fairness, and equity; these are the assumptions that drive any human rights agenda. By contrast, the activism Jesus engaged in has direct benefit to human beings, but its primary focus is to glorify God. The work Jesus did, His miracles, His sermons, and His incessant conflicts with the religious authorities, were for the purpose of lifting our gaze from ourselves to our God. It is by keeping our eyes on God and not ourselves that we find victory over sin, and the human condition is changed. Let's take a look at the words and deeds of Jesus through the lens of Biblical Christianity.

The first recorded miracle of Jesus was done at the wedding in Cana which was attended by Jesus, His mother, and His disciples. The wine ran out at the wedding, which was an awkward and even embarrassing situation for the newly married couple. As a member of the triune God, Jesus could have provided wine for every wedding or every person who needed wine, but He performed this miracle at a wedding where His actions could be observed by a large crowd. The point of the miracle was not to provide wine for the guests, or to rescue the couple from an awkward or embarrassing situation; Jesus turned water into wine to demonstrate the power and glory of God.

Jesus fed 5,000 in one instance, and then 4.000 in a separate instance, but the goal of these miracles was not to end hunger. Jesus could have provided enough food for everyone in His immediate vicinity or for everyone on the planet, but He did not. Jesus performed this miracle to demonstrate the awesome power of God. Jesus healed the sick and gave sight to the blind, but the purpose was not to end blindness and sickness. We know this because God is omnipotent, and as such, He could have eradicated all sickness and infirmity for all time, but He did not. Jesus healed the sick and gave sight to the blind in a very public forum where He could demonstrate the power of God.

The Weightier Matters

Let's observe the words of Jesus in Matthew 23:23 where He says, "***Woe to you, scribes and Pharisees, hypocrites! For you tithe mint and dill and cummin and have neglected the weightier provisions of the law; justice and mercy and faithfulness; but these things you should have done without neglecting the others***." Knowing the context of this verse is important to understanding what Jesus said. Throughout the entirety of chapter 23, Jesus is making a statement about hypocrisy and priorities. Jesus gave one woe after another, laying out what the religious authorities did as opposed to what they ought to have done. In this way, Jesus exposed the truth that their hearts and their actions were not in alignment with the piety they professed.

Jesus challenged the assumptions the religious leaders held about the law by revealing their hypocrisy. The scribes and Pharisees had no problem tithing the material things required by the law, and they enjoyed letting everyone know they had fulfilled those requirements, but Jesus was not making a case for social justice. Jesus was pointing out that both tithing and social justice are required by the law, but the weightier (More important) of the two is justice, mercy, and faithfulness.

Jesus was saying, yes, you should tithe, but a godly life must include a balance, which includes what we give to God, and how the love of God motivates us to treat others with justice, mercy, and faithfulness. Jesus was drawing a contrast between the things the scribes and Pharisees valued and the things they should have valued. If the scribes and Pharisees really cared about honoring God and fulfilling His law, they would have aligned their priorities with the priorities of God, which are:

1. **Justice** – Judging fairly and impartially according to the law
2. **Mercy** – Compassion, forgiveness, empathy for fellow sinners
3. **Faithfulness** – Fealty to God, and perseverance in doing what is right

The above three virtues are an outpouring of the great commandment to love God and to love others, but the primary focus is on the One who empowers and sustains us.

At this point you may wonder how we reconcile the truth that, "***God so loved the world, He gave His only begotten Son***", (John 3:16) with, "***There is none good but One, that is God***". (Mark 18:18) The main impediment to understanding this apparent paradox is our natural inclination to think transactionally. When we hear that God loved the world, (Humanity) so much that He gave His only begotten Son, we either elevate the value of human beings or diminish the value of God's Son, because in our minds the books must balance at the end of the transaction. We reason that only two things of relatively equal value can or should be exchanged. This is often why people dismiss Christianity: they cannot reconcile getting something for nothing, or, by contrast, they cannot accept living a life of service for unworthy human beings.

We must avoid a Christianity built on the humanist worldview, which says that people are inherently good, the books are balanced, and Jesus is the broker of the transaction. The problem is that if one conducts an honest search for goodness and worthiness in human beings, one will not find it. Even in the very best of human beings, we cannot find the goodness that we see in God. Hence, Mark 18:18. Once we accept that we are not worthy of God's love and that, for reasons we may never understand, He loves us despite our unworthiness, the Great Commandment to love God and love others will begin to make sense.

True, biblical Christianity inspires us to love others through acts of justice, mercy, and faithfulness, but not because ***people*** are good; we do this because ***God*** is good, because we are submitted to Him, and because we are committed to pleasing Him. When activism to promote justice, mercy, and faithfulness is built on the belief that people are good, we find ourselves in the trap of humanism, which can never justify or sustain our good works because people, apart from God, are not good, and they will always disappoint.

As the disciples walked with Jesus, their core beliefs were dramatically reshaped. The disciples witnessed Jesus doing and saying things that were simply out of alignment with everything they had been taught their entire lives. Jesus was not the least bit reluctant to point out the flaws in people, but His unbridled love for humanity despite these flaws was inescapable.

I next want us to take a look at what the disciples witnessed as Jesus dealt with two different women He encountered. If we really want to engage in effective, theocentric activism in this day, understanding the encounter Jesus had with the Syrophoenician woman, and the Samaritan woman are an excellent foundation on which to build our activism.

The Syrophoenician Woman

For the most part, Jesus confined His ministry to the region of Israel occupied by the Jewish people. However, interesting things happened when He ventured beyond those territories into the land of Canaan and when He went up to Samaria. We will first look at the interaction between Jesus and the Syrophoenician woman of Canaan, but for the sake of setting the context, let's consider what occurred between Matthew 14:13 and Matthew 15:21, where Jesus encountered the Syrophoenician woman:

- Jesus fed 5,000.
- Jesus sent the disciples to cross the Sea of Galilee.
- Jesus went up on the mountain by Himself to pray.
- Jesus walked on the water.
- Peter joined Jesus on the water, but he began to sink because of his lack of faith.
- Jesus was questioned by the Pharisees because His disciples violated their ritual hand-washing tradition.
- Jesus used the confrontation with the Pharisees to teach the crowds about true religion and true faith.

- Jesus went to the district of Tyre and Sidon, which is where He encountered the Syrophoenician woman. (Matthew 14:13-15:20)

Feeding 5,000 people, walking on water, and teaching on the law, were all examples of Jesus using powerful miracles and direct refutation of the Pharisaic doctrine to demonstrate the power of God and His covenant with the chosen people. However, the encounter with the Syrophoenician woman is a pivotal point in the time Jesus spent on earth because this is when Jesus began to expand His ministry and it became more inclusive of all humanity. The disciples, like all Jews, believed that Yahweh was theirs exclusively.

Since Moses led the Hebrew people into the promised land, they had grown accustomed to an us versus them mentality and given their struggle to possess the land and hold on to it, their defensive posture is understandable. However, going all the way back to Abram, we know that it was God's plan from the beginning to bless all people through the Jews. (Genesis 12:3) Although there were instances wherein Jesus healed non-Jewish people prior to His encounter with the Syrophoenician woman, it was during this encounter that Jesus openly addressed the scope of His ministry.

As a Christian, the recipient of God's incredible grace, it is important for me to ask why I, a man who is not a Jew, has been redeemed. While this is not a book on Christian theology, we are interested in learning how those who walked with Jesus were impacted by His words and His deeds. In this case, the disciples saw and heard Jesus move from a ministry that had until that point been focused exclusively on the Jewish people, to an inclusive ministry where non-Jews could enter into the grace of God through faith.

In Luke 7:1-10 we see that Jesus healed the servant of a Roman centurion, but the centurion sent other Jews to petition Jesus on behalf of his servant. In addition, the centurion had already proven himself to be an ally of the Jews. However, there was nothing in the interaction with the centurion that implied Jesus had shifted His ministry to include Gentiles. The encounter with the Centurion was a situation that stood alone, but the encounter with the Syrophoenician woman was entirely different. This woman approached Jesus herself, and unlike the centurion, she had no standing whatsoever among the Jewish people. Knowing all of this, Jesus baited the woman masterfully, and the resulting conversation was by divine providence.

The woman, knowing who Jesus was, cried out," Have mercy on me, Lord, Son of David; my daughter is cruelly demon-possessed." It is telling that nearly every encounter Jesus had with the religious authorities up to that point indicated that they either did not know who Jesus was or they simply rejected his claim to be the chosen messiah, but this woman called out to Jesus not only with complete knowledge of who He was, but with faith in what He could do. Therefore, if she was not informed by the religious authorities, and she was not a Jew following Jesus, where or from whom did she gain her understanding of what Jesus could do? It seems to me that even though she was not a Jew, like the centurion, the good news of Jesus could not be and was never intended to be confined to the Jews alone. Like many unsaved people today, the Syrophoenician woman heard about the savior, and she needed what He had to offer.

Initially, Jesus did not respond to the woman, but then His disciples, believing He should have nothing to do with the woman, urged Him to send her away. Now that Jesus had everyone focused on the issue at hand, He spoke not to His disciples, but directly to the woman, saying, "***I was sent only to the lost sheep of the house of Israel, (The Jewish people)"***. The woman persisted, bowing down, she said, "***Lord, help me!***" Jesus said to her, "***It is not good to take the children's bread and throw it to the dogs.***" I want to stop there for a moment. Jesus was not calling the woman a dog; He was giving her the opportunity to speak, not so much to Him, but to everyone listening. Jesus was giving this Syrophoenician woman the opportunity to explain that God finds value in the redemption of all human beings, and He does not dismiss anyone as insignificant. Hearing the Syrophoenician's response, Jesus said, "***O woman, your faith is great, it shall be done for you as you wish."***

Jesus did not learn anything new from the Syrophoenician woman, and He did not change His mind because of her. It was always in the plan of Jesus to expand His ministry, but it was also in His plan to start with Israel because it is the responsibility, the burden, and the privilege of God's chosen people to propagate the gospel. The Syrophoenician woman only provided Jesus with a powerful means of making His point.

Remember what happened in Matthew 10:5-15 when Jesus sent the disciples out. Jesus said, "***Do not go in the way of the Gentiles, and do not enter any city of the Samaritans***." Then, at the end of His earthly ministry, in Matthew 28:19, Jesus said, "***Go therefore and make disciples of all the nations, baptizing them in the name of the Father and the Son and the Holy Spirit***." The Greek word "*Gentiles*" used in Matthew 10 means people other than Jews. The Greek word we translate as nations in Matthew 28 is ethne, from which we get our English word ethnic. In Matthew 10, Jesus instructed His disciples not to preach to anyone other than Jews, but in Matthew 28:19, He instructed them and us to go to all people groups.

One of the ways we can outline the ministry of Jesus is:

1. **Revelation** – Jesus revealed to Israel that He is the promised Messiah.
2. **Indoctrination** – Jesus taught Israel how to correctly interpret the scriptures
3. **Proliferation** – Jesus sent Israel out to fulfill God's plan to bless the world

The encounter with the Syrophoenician woman was the transition from indoctrination to proliferation. The encounter with the Syrophoenician woman allowed Jesus to get His disciples' attention and understand that the ministry focus was expanding, but the apex of His ministry occurred in Matthew 28:19 when He gave them instructions to go into the entire world and preach to all people groups. Once His disciples understood their holistic call to love all people as God does, and to spread the gospel to the world, the stage was set for Jesus to leave the world, which is described in Acts chapter one. Everything we read in Acts was the culmination of events initiated during the interaction between Jesus and the Syrophoenician woman.

The woman at the well

When King Solomon died, his son Rehoboam reigned in his place. Rehoboam was the last king to reign over a united Israel. Soon after his reign began, the kingdom split with Jeroboam reigning as king of the 10 tribes that made up the northern kingdom of Israel, and Rehoboam as king of the remaining two tribes, which made up the southern kingdom of Judah. The line of succession from David remained intact in Judah through Zedekiah, the last king, but power in the northern kingdom was transferred from one monarch to another through a series of coups and intrigues. In 882 BC, King Omri purchased a hill from Shemer and named it Samaria, establishing it as the capital city of the Northern Kingdom of Israel.

Following the Assyrian conquest and occupation of Israel, the Jews who remained in the land intermarried with the Assyrians, and the people who emerged from these marriages became the despised Samaritans whom the Jews regarded as impure and unworthy. This group of people remained through the Assyrian, Persian, and Roman occupations of the land, and by the first century, when Jesus walked the earth, most Jews would go to great lengths to circumnavigate Samaria as they traveled from Judea to Galilee. The decision to travel directly from Judea through Samaria to get to Galilee was avoidable, yet deliberate. One way to look at John 4:4, which says, "***And He had to pass through Samaria***," is to say that in order to encounter the woman at the well, Jesus had to go through Samaria. Going through Samaria offered Jesus an opportunity to interact with a group of people who needed to hear the gospel.

Jesus reached out to the Samaritans on another journey as He traveled toward Jerusalem. In this situation, which was recorded in Luke 9:52, Jesus sent messengers ahead, and they entered a village of the Samaritans to make arrangements for Him. Unfortunately, Jesus was rejected by the Samaritans, and His disciples wanted to call down fire from heaven to destroy them because of their rejection, but Jesus told them He did not come to destroy men but to save them. We cannot be certain which incident came first, the one in Luke 9:52 or the one in John 4:7 but I think it is likely the encounter recorded in Luke came first because when Jesus encountered the men of Samaria in Luke He was met by hardened hearts and rejection, but as we will see, after His encounter with the woman at the well in John 4:7, the people of Samaria became believers.

As was the case during His encounter with the Syrophoenician woman, the conversation Jesus had with the Samaritan woman left no room for an isolationist, exclusionary doctrine, which supports inward-focused ministry. One of the first things I notice about the discussion between Jesus and the Samaritan woman is that Jesus presented Himself as someone in need of something she could give, when in fact it was Jesus who had something, the woman desperately needed.

Ministering to people by meeting their needs is a common practice, but Jesus presenting Himself as a person in need makes perfect sense because asking for assistance can be empowering and disarming at the same time. For example, a hungry person who comes to a church for food assumes they will have to pay for their meal by listening to someone preach to them, and they feel powerless over their circumstances because they are in need of what someone else has to offer them. However, people are more relaxed and feel more in control when they are the benefactor rather than the beneficiary. Asking the woman for a drink allowed her to lay aside any defensiveness and emboldened her to ask Jesus why He was even speaking to her. This presented Jesus with the perfect opportunity to let the woman know who He is, and what He had to offer her.

The Samaritan woman was at the well at a time when the other women of the village were not there. She was a woman who was likely ostracized because of her multiple relationships with men, so going to the well when the other women of the village drew water was not a viable option for her. Contemporary activism would focus on changing the way people think about the woman's lifestyle, creating a more acceptable and normal perception of her, but Jesus did not attempt to elevate her status within society, either as a woman or as a Samaritan. There was no advocacy for social change or for laws that would allow the woman to go to the well at a more convenient time. Jesus did not create an awareness campaign to redefine the woman's promiscuity as healthy, good, and normal. Jesus didn't even attempt to build the woman's self-esteem; in fact, rather than excuse or accept her behavior, Jesus called attention to her serial monogamy. Just as it was with the Syrophoenician woman, Jesus helped this woman to see herself as God sees her, which emboldened and excited her as she realized that she was a child of God, imperfect, but loved, nonetheless.

When we examine the ministry of Jesus, we find a distinct difference between His activism and modern activism. While modern activism centers on raising the status of certain groups within society to improve their lives here on earth, the activism of Jesus is about opening the hearts of all people so that they can experience abundant life now and eternal life after death. Modern activism focuses on changing government, institutions, and the way society regards marginalized groups by normalizing sinful behavior and meeting immediate, felt needs.

The goal of this modern activism is to elevate the status of these groups within society, but Jesus focuses on changing the hearts of people and revealing the image of God within them. This is not only the distinction between the ministry of Jesus and modern activism, but it is also the energy that fuels true evangelism. People are not converted by affirming and asserting their own self-worth, but by discovering the infinite value of the eternal God who loves them and finds value in their lives. Therefore, we don't feed the poor and clothe the naked because of their intrinsic value to society; we do these things because it is beneath the dignity of our humanity as children of God to treat them any other way.

I have no interest in minimizing the work of Martin Luther King, Ceazar Chavez, Mahatma Gandhi, Mother Theresa, Nelson Mandela, or any other modern-day activist, but I do want to make clear the distinction between the impetus, methods, and outcomes of these people and those of Jesus. The essential difference is found in the words of Jesus to the Samaritan woman at the well. "***Everyone who drinks of this water will thirst again; but whoever drinks of the water that I will give him shall never thirst; but the water that I will give him will become in him a well of water springing up to eternal life***." (John 4:13-14)

The successes of the American civil rights movement were limited by the law and our constitution, and as such, these successes remain in peril and must be continually defended. Mother Theresa dedicated her life to feeding the hungry people of Calcutta, India, and as bountiful as her work was, the people are still hungry. Nelson Mandela helped to end Apartheid in South Africa, and he helped to reshape that nation, but the struggle for equity in South Africa continues. The proliferation of the gospel is the activism of Jesus, and the effects of the gospel on individuals, families, communities, nations, and the world are eternal. People who accept the gospel of Jesus will experience hunger, they will be ostracized, they will experience oppression of all sorts, but their lives will be full, their eternity will be undeniably secure, and that is the activism of Jesus.

The least of these

Activism is all about changing things from the way they are to the way they ought to be. So far in this chapter, we have focused on motivation and the result of activism. In this segment, I want to redirect our attention to the role activism played in Jesus advancing the plan of God. For this, we need to revisit the creation narrative found in Genesis. Without a firm grasp of the Old Testament, which lays the foundation for the gospels, the Acts, the epistles, and the Revelation, it is difficult to develop a holistic understanding of the role activism has played in God's plan.

When I was about seven, I took a few piano lessons, and I recall the piano teacher showing me a strange, squiggly-looking mark on the sheet music called a rest. I remember wondering how playing piano could be so exhausting that I would need to take a break in the middle of the song. My teacher explained that the rest was put there to indicate intervals where the musician was to simply stop playing. It was decades later that I realized rest and exhaustion do not necessarily go hand in hand. Life, in some respects, is like a musical composition played by an orchestra. If everyone played at the same time all the time, the music would be chaotic and meaningless. Like a musician playing in an orchestra, sometimes in life we rest simply because we need a cessation of activity in preparation for our next movement, and to allow other elements of the composition to move to the forefront.

The first chapter of Genesis tells the creation story, and it describes how God created the universe in six days, but on the seventh day He rested. I used to imagine God working hard for six days, and then on the seventh day He sat down on a rock, wiped His brow, sighed, and then rested His exhausted body. But of course, that is not what happened. God did not rest because He was exhausted; He allowed Himself a cessation of activity in preparation for His next movement and to appreciate what He had accomplished. God gave us the sabbath to model His approach to work, and He expects us to rest from our usual daily activity of production after six days of work just as He did. However, over time, the legalists made a series of rules and regulations around the sabbath that had nothing to do with its original intent.

When Jesus began to draw attention to what the religious authorities had done to the sabbath, His purpose was to bring us back into alignment with God's intentions and to challenge anything with a pretense of piety that did not glorify God. Jesus exposed ceremonial washing for the vain, empty practice that it was. (Luke 11:37-41) Jesus also exposed the Pharisees' false reverence for the sabbath by deliberately healing in direct violation of their sabbath regulations. There is no doubt that Jesus had compassion for the people he healed, but He wanted people to understand that the sabbath was God's gift to humanity; it was not intended as a burden or to create systemic cruelty and indifference toward His people. (Mark 2:27-28)

Liberation Theology, Woke Christianity, and the resistance

There is a raging debate taking place between White evangelical Christianity on the right and Christian social activism on the left. Defending the righteousness of modern Western Christianity, evangelicals like Owen Strachan dig deep into their theology to dismiss or even besmirch any movement that demands a reckoning for injustices perpetrated by misguided Christians of the past. While Christian Theologian James H. Cone argued in the late 1960s that Black Theology is "***The heart of the Christian gospel***." Regardless of the merits and mishaps of these polarized positions, there is an agenda at work in each perspective that misses the mark of the Christian gospel. Both positions fail to recognize that the Bible was never intended to condemn the American social system or to exonerate those who have benefited from it.

The most important and God-honoring thing I can say about any Christian activism from the right or the left comes in the form of a warning: ***Beware of the agendas***. So many well-intentioned people have seen injustice and felt compelled to drag Jesus and the gospel into their struggle. Since man rebelled against God in the garden, sin and its offspring, injustice, have tormented humanity. In a quest for relief from these two spiritual terrorists, sin and injustice, we have turned to all manner of false gods and false religion, but history has revealed that anytime we try to fit God into our agendas or treat Christianity like a tool to be used in advancing our agendas, we make a mess of things.

Liberation Theology uses Christianity as a means to an end; I would argue it's a noble end, yet it misappropriates the Word of God and the Christian faith for the sake of man. Woke Christianity reduces the gospel to such a degree that the gospel becomes almost irrelevant as it attempts to dethrone the dominant race in America to elevate the oppressed.

As we have seen with the civil rights movement in America, it is only a short matter of time before the LGBTQ movement attaches itself to Liberation Theology, Black

Liberation Theology, and Woke Christianity. The gospel - the good news that the Messiah has come, is about abundant life now and the eternity of the human soul. As lovers of Christ, we would do well to keep God at the center of our theology while allowing the Holy Spirit to guide us in ancillary social issues as the fruit of our Christianity. This is not to say that Christians should not be activists for social justice. God calls us to champion the cause of Justice and Christians ought to engage in social justice reform, but we should never confuse our human activism with the primary purpose of the Bible, which is to direct our gaze upward and into eternity.

Remember what Jesus said when asked by the Pharisees, "***What is the greatest commandment***?" Jesus said, "***You shall love the Lord your God with all your heart and with all your soul, and with all your mind. This is the great and foremost commandment. The second is like it, you shall love your neighbor as yourself.***" (Matthew 22:36-40) The great commandment simplifies theology. Anything we do or say that does not demonstrate love for God with all our heart, soul, and mind, and anytime we do not love our neighbor as ourselves, we fall short of the great commandment, and our faith is useless. Paul doubled down on this when he said that anything we do with the appearance of godliness, without love, is worthless. (1 Corinthians 13:1-3) Therefore, everything we do and say must meet this standard.

The strengths and weaknesses of arguments on the right or the left must hold up to the standard ensconced within the great commandment to love God and love others. Therefore, to ignore, diminish, dismiss, or defend any group's complicity in systems of oppression is ungodly because it is dishonest and it is unloving toward the oppressed. Jesus would never have ignored or denied the suffering of any group caused by another, regardless of whether the injustice occurred historically or is occurring contemporaneously. On the other hand, to misappropriate the Word of God to condemn an entire race of people because the sins of their ancestors have given them an unfair advantage over others is ungodly. This condemnation is ungodly because it is dishonest, and it fails to demonstrate the grace of God.

Jesus never overlooked the sins of the past, but He held people accountable for their own sins, not the sins of their ancestors. Even when Jesus mentioned the historical sins of the religious authorities, He did so in connection with their own sinful behavior, not to hold them accountable for the sins of their forebearers. As Christians, we have to hold firm to the fact that the Word of God is not intended to defend the behavior or the theology of men; the ***Word*** of God is for the ***plan*** of God. Jesus understood this, and as Christians, we also ought to understand this.

Seeing life through God colored glasses

The first of the ten commandments brought down from Sinai by Moses said, "***I am the Lord your God, who brought you out of the land of Egypt, out of the house of slavery. You shall have no other gods before Me.***" As a new Christian, I wondered why God insists that we put Him at the center of our lives. I came from a secular worldview where equality was valued, and this did not feel equal or fair, so I was perplexed. It wasn't long before I came to understand why God wants us to make Him our priority above all other things; it's because God and only God can say to every living person, there is nothing better for you than Me. Everything we do in devotion to God makes us better and improves our lives; every act of worshiping God strengthens us in ways we will never know this side of heaven. Therefore, treating ourselves as equals with God is detrimental to our own being.

As Jesus healed the sick, gave sight to the blind, fed the hungry, advocated for the defenseless, and challenged the religious authorities, He redirected the gaze of those who walked with Him from the plight of humanity toward the glory of God. Through His acts of service, Jesus showed His followers that when we make an idol out of ourselves or when we make an idol out of humanity, we diminish our own value. (Mark 10:36-45) Jesus taught His followers that serving others benefits the one serving more than the one being served, it is this revelation within us that resonates with the Spirit of God. This is the heart and the essence of Christian activism; understanding that we serve because we are created in the image of God. (Genesis 1:26)

Too much time and energy have been devoted to looking at ourselves and then trying to imagine what God looks like when we should be looking at God to see what we ought to look like. Of course, God is spirit and has no physical form, which means the things that make us image bearers of God are not physical but spiritual. Therefore, when we serve, defend, pray for, and love others (The great commandment), we reflect the image of God, which in turn draws us closer to God, which in turn gives meaning to our lives. This is why Paul said, "***In everything I showed you that by working hard in this manner you must help the weak and remember the words of the Lord Jesus, that He Himself said, it is more blessed to give than to receive.***" (Acts 20:35)

Redirecting our eyes to God brings value to our lives by daily conforming us to the image of God. This is what Jesus wanted His followers to see, not the miracles but the God of the miracles, not the rage against systems of oppression, but the inherent dignity of being made in God's image, which makes us emissaries of God through our capacity to care for others!

Those who followed Jesus as He ministered here on earth were aware of Genesis 1:26, but just like we see a White Jesus in American churches today, or just like Black Liberation Theology would posit an African American image of Jesus, 1st century Jews likely assumed that God would look like a Hebrew man, and the Messiah would look the same. However, Genesis 1:26 was never intended to give us an idea of what God looks like physically; it is a scripture that helps us see our capacity to mirror the loving and just attributes of God.

In August 1963, Martin Luther King penned the Letter from a Birmingham Jail. The letter, which was originally handwritten, is 6 ½ typed pages long, and in it, King references ancient Greek scholars, theologians from the 14th century like Martin Luther, and prominent twentieth-century thinkers. In this letter written to several members of the 1963 clergy, including Catholics, Protestants, and Jews, King makes a strong morality-based case for social justice. Using Augustine himself as his witness, Dr. King condemns immoral laws as well as Christian apathy. However, King never made an exegetical case from scripture for social justice.

Exegesis draws meaning and mandates from the Bible which helps us to discern God's will, which defines Christian morality and gives us direction. God's Word, properly understood, supplants human morality. I must restate my thesis; I am grateful for the work of Martin Luther King and other civil rights leaders. In my humble human opinion, these leaders did the right thing, but that doesn't necessarily mean their words and actions were biblical mandates.

In 21st-century America, our form of government is a representative republic. Our founding documents have lofty ideas of a government by the people and for the people, but democracy is complicated, clumsy, frustrating, imperfect, and ultimately unsatisfying. The work of Martin Luther King was necessary because:

- Although our constitution should have made slavery illegal, chattel slavery continued for 400 years
- Although the 14th amendment should have ended Jim Crow when Plessy Vs Ferguson was argued before the US Supreme Court, it took the 1954 Brown vs Board of Education decision to effectively end Jim Crow.
- Although we have lofty ideas expressed in the preamble to the constitution which declare that all men are created equal, it took the 1964 Voting Rights Act to legally address poll taxes and other means of voter suppression.

If the path toward seeing the image of God in humanity was through the law of man, why did we struggle, and why do we continue to struggle to treat one another with dignity and love?

In 1982, I was working as a security guard at the Greyhound bus depot in Downtown Minneapolis. Part of my job at the bus depot was to stand outside the terminal and greet passengers as they disembarked from the buses. I was a young man who had been raised by a mother who understood the civil rights movement; she taught my siblings and me about segregation in the deep south and about violence against Blacks.

One spring day, a bus from Natchez, Mississippi, pulled in to the depot, and the weary passengers began to disembark. The last passenger to get off the bus was an elderly Black woman who looked to be in her eighties. When she saw me, she walked straight to me and asked the strangest question. Through parched lips, she asked, "***Do you know where a colored person can get a drink of water***?" Although legal segregation in America had ended in 1954 with the landmark Brown vs Board of Education Supreme Court decision, this poor soul, who had been living in the deep south her entire life, was unaffected by the change in the law because in her heart, there was still reason to fear Jim Crow.

Moses led the Hebrew people out of Egypt because God had orchestrated events that eventually changed the law that had enslaved the people, but even though they had been emancipated, they continued to behave as enslaved people. It took 40 years of wandering in the wilderness for the Hebrew people to walk in freedom. The Emancipation Proclamation was signed in 1863, but even after a bloody civil war, both the freed slaves and the slave owners continued to live as though some vestige of slavery remained. We now have a federal holiday to commemorate the reality that freed slaves continued to live as slaves even after their emancipation, and yet, nearly 30 years after segregation was legally ended in America, an old woman, born and raised in the south, got off that bus in Minneapolis, still afraid that Jim Crow was alive and well. Laws do not change the human heart; only God can do that.

The greatest and most dramatic emancipation in the Bible is the exodus, but God did not free the Hebrew slaves for life, liberty, and the pursuit of happiness. God led the Hebrews out of slavery so they could pursue lives of worship and so that through them, all people would be blessed. (Genesis 12:3) Four hundred and thirty years later, God orchestrated events that led the Hebrew people back into bondage, and He did so for the same reason: to create in them a disciplined life of worship so they could fulfill their divine purpose. Another 500 years later, we saw the advent of Jesus, and the greatest misconception the Jews had about Jesus was that He came to emancipate them from Roman rule, but that was not His agenda. Jesus spent three years on earth developing disciples (Students) into apostles (Teachers) so they could fulfill their divine calling to lead others to God.

As I mentioned earlier in this section, activism is all about changing things from the way they are to the way they ought to be. Secular social justice movements fight to change laws, government, and public opinion, from the way they are to the way humans think they ought to be. Jesus fought to make God known and to reclaim His people for His purposes. A high view of scripture says the Word of God is sufficient to accomplish God's purposes, but like many modern activists, Dr. King forged alliances with other activists, organizations, and even with other faiths, drawing on the strength of the collective.

I am reminded of the Latin phrase, ***sola scriptura, sola fide, and sola gratia,*** which means, by scripture alone, by faith alone, and by grace alone. This Latin phrase, in many ways, was the battle cry of the Protestant Reformation, which gave birth to all denominations within the universal church. The term protestant is a derivative of the word protest, so the multiple denominations we now see within the universal church are literally the result of the 14th-century reformer,

Martin Luther's protest against the Catholic (Universal) church.

Although the protestant church was built on a strong foundation of protest against a catholic church which failed to subordinate itself to the authority of scripture, over one half century after his assassination, the Reverend Dr. Martin Luther King is remembered by most people around the world as a secular activist, and few people can site a single thing he said or did that brought them closer to biblical Christianity or the image of God. While I am not criticizing King's work, I wonder if his legacy as an apostle of Jesus would have been more enduring if he had patterned his activism after the approach of Jesus, which is to change hearts by directing people to the image of God from which we are created, rather than taking an inclusive, ecumenical approach to his work.

Like a pendulum swinging to and fro, Laws, governments, and opinions change, but the most effective and enduring activism occurs when people are motivated by something greater than themselves. This is the model of activism Jesus demonstrated for those who followed Him. It is important for us to appreciate the difference between the activism of Jesus and that of modern secular activists because when we conflate these two, we weaken the gospel. As Christians, we must zealously guard the historical Jesus or we begin to contour the image of God to the image of man, and we dare not allow that to happen.

Chapter Ten

Messiah

For this final chapter, we consider Jesus as the Messiah. The Hebrew word for Messiah is Mashiach, which means "Anointed One". The Greek equivalent of Mashiach is Christos, from which we get the word Christ. Both words convey the idea of one anointed to lead the people of God. We will again put ourselves in the position of those who walked alongside Jesus as He fulfilled the messianic prophesies.

Humanity has been in need of a messiah from the moment sin was ushered into existence in the Garden of Eden. God promised a deliverer, one who would provide a means of restoring our relationship with Him, and He Himself is the fulfillment of that promise in the person of Jesus. The questions we will entertain in this chapter are, how did those in Jesus's inner circle respond to being in the presence of the one who fulfilled all prophesies of the promised Messiah, and how was this aspect of His being revealed to others?

All of humanity, regardless of religion or faith, looks for, longs for, and lives for, hope. As Christians, we confess that our hope is in Jesus Christ. The Old Testament prophets preached and wrote during the time when kings reigned over the Northern Kingdom of Israel and the Southern Kingdom of Judah. The prophets issued warnings to the kings and the people, telling them about the consequences of sin, but they also gave hope for a messiah who would lead God's people. The prophets Daniel, Jeremiah, and Isaiah are quoted frequently in the New Testament, and Isaiah in particular is quoted by Jesus Himself. (Luke 4:18-19) It is with the words of Isaiah that Jesus established Himself as the promised messiah early in His ministry.

> *The spirit of the Lord is upon me, because He anointed me to preach the gospel to the poor. He has sent me to proclaim release to the captives, and recovery of sight to the blind, to set free those who are oppressed, to proclaim the favorable year of the Lord. – Isaiah 61:1-2*

Each of the four gospel writers, Matthew, Mark, Luke, and John, takes a unique approach to writing their account of the life of Jesus, and each has their own agenda. Matthew's gospel has a heavy emphasis on the Jewish identity of Jesus. Mark presents Jesus as the suffering servant. Luke the physician is primarily concerned with the humanity of Jesus, and John places special emphasis on the deity of Jesus. As such, we can observe that the gospel of Matthew begins with a lengthy genealogy that goes all the way back to Abraham, the progenitor of the Jewish faith. Mark begins with a recitation of Malachi 3:1, where the prophet previews the ministry of Jesus as one of service to humanity. Luke begins his gospel with a narrative describing the conception, gestation, and birth of Jesus, and John begins by establishing that Jesus has always existed as God and that Jesus is the creator of all things.

In previous chapters, we had to wait until Jesus was fully grown to determine the effect He had on those within His inner circle. In this chapter, we will see how others responded to Jesus as Messiah in-utero. As previously mentioned, by trade, Luke was a physician, a man curious about human physiology, so it is no surprise that of the four gospel writers, it was Luke who went into the most detail about the conception, gestation, birth, early infancy, and childhood of Jesus. In fact, Luke is the only gospel writer who provides us with any insight at all into the childhood and early adolescence of Jesus. As one who was uniquely interested in presenting Jesus as fully human, Luke is the only gospel writer who gave us a look at the effect Jesus had on those around Him before He was born.

The Great Birth Announcement

Each year during the Christmas season, I take time to read the Christmas story as it is told in Luke chapters one and two. There is so much going on in these two chapters, but I want to focus on:

- The conversation between the angel Gabriel and Zacharias
- The conversation between the angel Gabriel and Mary
- The conversation between Mary and Elizabeth
- The reaction of Herod

The Conversation Between The Angel Gabriel And Zacharias

In anticipation of and in preparation for the birth of Jesus, Gabriel first appeared to Zacharias, a descendant of Levi and a priest in the temple. It is important to note that Gabriel did not appear to Zacharias's wife, Elizabeth; he appeared to Zacharias. We will touch on why this is important when we get to the conversation between Mary and Elizabeth. Zacharias and Elizabeth were very old, and they had no offspring. Gabriel told Zacharias that his wife Elizabeth would conceive a child in her old age, and that the child would play a significant role in the life of the coming Messiah. As a Levite, one who was knowledgeable about the ancient scriptures, Zacharias would have been very familiar with the story of Abraham and Sarah, who were also blessed with a child in their old age. However, Zacharias did not respond to Gabriel as one who understood and believed the scriptures.

Upon hearing the message delivered by Gabriel, Zacharias said, "***How will I know this for certain? For I am an old man and my wife is advanced in years.***" Gabriel's response was, ***"I am Gabriel, who stands in the presence of God, and I have been sent to speak to you and to bring you this good news. And behold, you shall be silent and unable to speak until the day when these things take place, because you did not believe my words, which will be fulfilled in their proper time***."

Zacharias's question, ***how will I know this for certain*** was tantamount to saying, I do not believe. But Zacharias should have believed because this was not the first time God had performed this particular miracle. The first time God created life from a lifeless womb, it resulted in the birth of Issac, the father of Jacob, the father of the 12 tribes of Israel. Zacharias was made mute because, although he should have believed, he did not. Sometimes it helps to read scripture with a little bit of imagination and attitude, so please indulge me for just a moment while I attempt to dramatize the scene where Gabriel speaks to Zacharias.

Basically, Zacharias said to God's messenger, "Hey Gabe, I don't believe a word you are saying." Now imagine the angel Gabriel standing in front of Zacharias with an expression of shock and anger, one hand on his hip, and the other hand waving a finger before Zacharias' face. Now with that image in mind, read Gabriel's words to Zacharias again. Look here, Zach, I don't know who you think you're talking to, (Okay, that's me taking a bit of artistic license). Anyway, Gabriel said to Zacharias, ***"I am Gabriel, who stands in the presence of God, and I have been sent to speak to you and to bring this good news."*** (Luke 1:19)

Zacharias had every reason to believe, and absolutely no reason to disbelieve, so Gabriel left no further room for doubt, he removed Zacharias's ability to utter another word until the good news he came to bring had come to pass. On a side note, there is a lesson for us in this interaction. When God gives you good news and makes you aware of how He has done in the past what He is promising to do for you in the present, believe Him so He doesn't need to go to extreme measures to make you believe.

After being struck mute, Zacharias communicated with his wife Elizabeth, probably through writing, and told her what Gabriel told him, but it is important to the story to understand that no one told either Zacharias or Elizabeth that Elizabeth's young cousin, probably a 2nd or 3rd cousin, was going to give birth to the Messiah. If Gabriel revealed this to Elizabeth, it was not recorded in scripture, but I am inclined to believe that this information was communicated directly to Elizabeth by God, and it happened the instant Mary appeared at Elizabeth's door. I believe that if Elizabeth had known that her young relative was going to give birth to the Messiah, Mary would not have had to go to Elizabeth; Elizabeth would have gone to Mary.

The conversation between the angel Gabriel and Mary

Mary was a young girl, about 13 years old, and engaged to Joseph, a carpenter. Gabriel appeared to Mary and explained that she would give birth to the Messiah. In response to this news, Mary asked a perfectly reasonable question, how can this be, since I am a virgin?" Although it is extremely rare for old women to conceive and give birth, it was not unprecedented at the time Mary spoke with Gabriel, but in the entire history of humanity, there had never been a virgin birth. Rather than saying to Gabriel, how can I know this, Mary asked, " ***How can this be***". Another way to put Mary's question is, what will be the process for this conception, since the normal means of conceiving a child requires me to be intimate with a man, and I have not been intimate with a man.

The difference between the responses of Zacharias and Mary is this; whereas Zacharias asked how he could know (Believe) what he was being told, Mary believed what she was being told; she only wanted to know *how* the events Gabriel spoke of would unfold. The emphasis of Zacharias's response was on how Gabriel's words could be believed, but belief was implicit in Mary's response.

Mary's response was full of incredible faith; with her simple question, "***How can this be?***", she acknowledged that God could make this happen. Part of the challenge with understanding Mary's question is due to our own experience with cultural idiomatic speech. When we hear the phrase, how can this be, doubt is implicit in how we hear the question because of our cultural context. When we say how can this be, it is not really a question, it is an indictment of untruth and a rhetorical statement which indicates the impossibility of what is being proposed, but that is not how Mary used this phrase.

If we remove our contemporary use of this phrase which is to point to an obvious impossibility, and look at what she actually said, we can see she was really asking Gabriel by what means she was going to get pregnant absent intimate relations with a man. When we ask a question like this in our current cultural context, we are assuming the question cannot be answered because someone has made an impossible proposition. Mary on the other hand was making no such assumption. Therefore, Gabriel explained the process of the immaculate conception to Mary, and when she heard the explanation, she believed and was at peace. Mary was so excited by what Gabriel explained that she packed a bag and went to visit her cousin Elizabeth to see the miracle God had done for her.

I think Mary's response to this news delighted the heart of God more than we can possibly know. God understands the limitations of our intellect; He created us. God knows that our capacity to believe is limited by our experience, and this is why faith endears us to God. Remember in chapter two, we looked at Hebrews 11:1, ***"Now faith is the substance of things hoped for, the evidence of things not seen."*** As Christians we willingly exchange substance and evidence for faith. Hebrews 11:9 goes on to inform us that without faith it is impossible to please God. When Mary heard the proclamation of God, spoken through Gabriel, she was convinced without demanding proof. Her reaction to the news was an exciting manifestation of faith. She did not require proof that she would give birth to a child; she only needed to know how it would occur and what her role would be. Once she heard that the Holy Spirit would come over her, which would result in her pregnancy, her immediate response was to run and tell Elizabeth.

The Conversation Between Mary And Elizabeth

Immediately following her conversation with Gabriel, Mary left for Judah, where Elizabeth lived. The journey from Galilee, where Mary was living, to Judah, where Elizabeth lived, was about 7-10 days long. At some point between the time Mary left Galilee and the time she arrived in Judah, both Elizabeth and her unborn son John became aware that Mary would give birth to the promised Messiah.

When Mary entered the home of Zacharias and Elizabeth, both the unborn child, John, and Elizabeth had incredible reactions to her presence. I think we have heard this story so many times that some of the salient details become hidden from us. Read Luke chapters one and two again and notice that no one, including the angel Gabriel, gave Elizabeth any information regarding Mary's pregnancy. Although it is not mentioned in scripture, there is a substantial likelihood that the two women had never actually met. They did not chat on the phone, or gather at family reunions, and they were not Facebook friends. Mary had been pregnant for no more than seven days when she arrived at Elizabeth's door, and even if someone else knew about Mary's pregnancy, it would have been impossible for anyone to have told Elizabeth about it prior to Mary's arrival. Scripture informs us that immediately upon hearing that she would become pregnant by the Holy Spirit, Mary made the seven-day journey to Judah. All of these facts make the reactions of both Elizabeth and her unborn child nothing short of amazing.

The unborn child leaped in the womb of his mother, and having been filled with the Holy Spirit, Elizabeth went on for 13 verses proclaiming how blessed Mary was to be chosen by God and to give birth to the Messiah. If Zacharias was somewhere in the background watching what took place between these two women, I can only imagine that he kicked himself for his feckless response to the good news he received from the angel Gabriel. These two women and the unborn child were full of faith, wonder, and praise, while Zacharias responded with skepticism. When we examine these scriptures, it becomes clear that even before Jesus was born, He was teaching, changing lives, and inspiring faith in those around Him.

The Reaction Of Herod And The Magi

This book is as much about the way Jesus's adversaries were impacted by Him as it is about those who followed and worshipped Him, and we will need to go to Matthew's gospel to see the reaction of Herod, King of Judea. It is truly shocking what powerful men will do to increase or to retain power. Herod's reaction to the news that a Jewish Messiah had been born was nothing new, and weak men continue to be threatened by the presence of Jesus to this day. Harod's act of infanticide was also not original in biblical history. When the Pharaoh of Egypt heard of a man who would lead the Hebrew people out of bondage, his solution to the problem was the same. (Exodus 1:15-16)

Before we dig into Herod's actions, I think we need to give some attention to the magi who arrived from the east to see the child who was born King of the Jews. The Magi were likely eastern astrologers who studied celestial bodies and unusual phenomena among the stars. These men saw a star and knew the Jewish prophecy of a powerful King who would be born to lead the Jews. The Magi followed the star, which took them to Jerusalem, where they were summoned by Herod, who asked them the exact time the star had appeared to them. After ascertaining the date when the star first appeared to the Magi, he sent them to Bethlehem in search of the child. Herod told the Magi to let him know where the child was so that he could go and worship Him.

Knowing the exact time the star appeared to the Magi allowed Herod to establish a time of birth so that he could determine how old the child was. This information would be valuable later when the Magi obeyed the voice of God and refused to tell Herod where the child was located. With this information, Herod determined that the child was two years old or younger. Therefore, not knowing the specific location of the child spoken of in Jewish prophecy, Herod had every male Jewish child two years old and younger killed. (Matthew 2:16-18)

Herod's reaction to the birth of Jesus was a vicious yet ultimately ineffective attempt to circumvent the will of God. Operating in the natural, Herod saw the world as men with power often do. Herod believed that he was in control and that he could manipulate events in his own favor, but regardless of the outcome, it is important to recognize the powerful and visceral reactions of both Herod and the Magi to the news that the Messiah had arrived. The Magi traveled across the known world to witness prophecy fulfilled and to worship the One whom the prophecy referred to. Herod gathered all his chief priests to learn where the Messiah would be born, and when that didn't work, he tried to trick the Magi into revealing the location of the Messiah. When all his schemes failed, Herod committed a shocking act of infanticide just to retain power and dash the hopes of the Jewish people. These polar opposite reactions are powerful examples of how the birth of Jesus the Messiah affected the world.

Simeon And Anna

Faith is prone to fragility, and God knows this. Many of us can recall times when we heard God's call clearly, and we knew without a doubt that He was directing our footsteps. Those of us who have heard God's call also know that the more important and challenging the call, the greater the chance for doubt. It's not that God doesn't compel us to do small things like take a right at a fork in the road, or to say yes when no is on the tip of your tongue, but when God calls us to do big, life-changing things, there is often a sense of awe that can morph into questioning the call. However, the most crucial point in the lifecycle of a calling from God is the period of time after we accept the call and when we begin to move according to His will.

Joseph and Mary had believed the angel of God who told them Mary would give birth to the Messiah; then they stepped out on faith and traveled to Bethlehem, where Jesus was born. Now the Magi were gone, the shepherds were gone, Gabriel was no longer speaking to them, and they traveled back to Jerusalem. Upon arriving at the temple, they had an amazing encounter with two older Jews sent by God.

With 20/20 hindsight, it is easy to see that this couple was on the verge of making history, but Joseph and Mary did not have our historical vantage point to see events unfolding; instead, they had faith, which is sometimes fragile. Joseph chose to believe that the child his bride had just given birth to was of divine origin, and Mary chose to believe that God had a plan for her child, but all of this was at that time unprecedented. Strong as their faith was, Joseph and Mary needed affirmation, and God provided.

Following the birth of Jesus, His circumcision on the eighth day, and Mary's purification period according to Levitical law, Mary and Joseph traveled about 5 miles from Bethlehem to the temple in Jerusalem to present baby Jesus before the Lord.

Simeon and Anna affirmed what Joseph and Mary already knew. The call on Simeon from God was to live until he had seen the Messiah face to face. It had been revealed to Simeon by the Holy Spirit that he would not see death before he had seen the Lord's Christ. (Luke 2:25) Moving in the Spirit, Simeon came into the temple, which means that he was compelled to enter the temple at that time by the Holy Spirit. This was a divine appointment; he was not there by chance. Knowing the fragility of faith, God had called Simeon to deliver a message to Joseph and Mary at that exact time. Seeing the baby, Simeon took Him into his arms, blessed God, and told the couple that God had given him a mission to minister to the couple at that specific time. (Luke 2:27-32)

God also sent a prophetess into the temple at that specific time. Anna was eighty-four years old and had been a widow for probably sixty-five years. She was married, likely when she was about 13 or 14 years old. She lived with her husband for 7 years until his death, and at the time she encountered Joseph and Mary with the baby Jesus, she was about eighty-four years old. Scripture says that Anna served in the temple day and night, fasting and praying. (Luke 2:36-38) At the moment Simeon made his proclamation, Anna began giving thanks to God, and she told everyone who was anticipating the redemption of Jerusalem that the Messiah had been born and that He was among them.

The reactions of both Simeon and Anna demonstrate the impact Jesus had even before He was able to speak, but what's more, these reactions inform us of the meticulous care God gave to heralding the arrival of His son. The Jewish people had been promised a Messiah, and they were greatly in need of one. The world was in need of a savior then as it is now. God has not only told us what He would do for our salvation, He supernaturally inspired those who surrounded Jesus long before Jesus delivered His first sermon or performed His first miracle.

Dealing With Difficult Passages

Pastor Voddie Baucham once said, "*Biblical illiteracy is rampant in the church.*" It is always my hope that anything I write will lead people into a deeper exploration of God's Word. I believe that an uninformed Christian can be very dangerous, and the cure is not found in commentaries, good sermons from gifted exegetical preachers, YouTube videos, or social media. The cure for Christian ignorance is to read and study the Bible for oneself. When we study the Bible, it is critical that we start with an affirmation that the Bible is the inspired, authoritative, inerrant, Word of God and that when we come to difficult passages we do not understand, we must prayerfully seek God's guidance, knowing that because the Bible was inspired by an omniscient God, it stands to reason that we will encounter passages that are at least for the moment, inaccessible to our limited intellect. We also need to accept that the Bible was not written with 21st-century America as its original audience. Therefore, if we really wish to understand the Bible, we have to be willing to consider what is written from the perspective of people who lived at a different time and in a different culture than our own.

The narratives in Matthew and Luke, which describe the birth and childhood of Jesus, can present a critical point of faith for those of us who believe in the inerrancy of scripture. Because of our American culture, we tend to expect storylines to flow chronologically and sequentially, but the Bible does not always bend to our will in these matters. Therefore, we must stand on our convictions that the Bible is indeed the inerrant Word of God. So herein lies the problem; Matthew's gospel records that the family of Jesus left Bethlehem and went to Egypt (Matthew 13-14) while Luke's gospel records that the family left Bethlehem and went to Jerusalem. (Luke 2:21-22) This leaves us with a quandary: which narrative is true? And why does there appear to be a contradiction if the Word of God is inerrant? In resolving this perplexity, it might help to ask if it is necessary for the problem to be resolved as either or as opposed to both and.

I offer the following proposition: It was about a five-mile walk from Bethlehem to Jerusalem. Because of this, it is possible that both gospels give an accurate account of what occurred, even if there is a divergence in the two narratives. It is possible that the family left Bethlehem, traveled to Jerusalem, presented the child in the temple per the Jewish custom, returned to Bethlehem, and then they were warned by the angel to flee to Egypt from Bethlehem. Remember, the emphasis of Matthew's gospel is on establishing Jesus as a Jew who fulfilled the prophecies of the coming Messiah. Jesus being called out of Egypt by an angel of the Lord following the death of Herod is a significant fulfillment of Jewish prophecy. Because Matthew wrote to a Jewish audience, he felt compelled to speak to this aspect of the narrative.

Luke was a physician (Col 4:14), and he was primarily interested in developing a narrative that presents Jesus as fully God while remaining fully human. As a physician, Luke emphasized the humanity of Jesus, and his gospel was written to Greeks and Hellenized Jews. Luke's audience needed to connect more with the humanity of Jesus than with His Jewish identity. Those for whom Luke wrote his gospel would not have been as familiar with or interested in the Jewish prophecy, "***Out of Egypt I have called my Son***". (Hosea 11:1) Therefore, Luke did not include this portion of the narrative.

Matthew included the flight to Egypt and, more importantly, the family's exodus from Egypt, but Luke included the visit to Jerusalem when Jesus was twelve years old and the encounter with Simeon and Anna. These portions of the narrative, while they do not affirm any of the Jewish prophesies, are very relatable to Luke's audience. Although neither the visit to the temple when Jesus was an infant, or when He was twelve years old involved any prophesy, they do give us a picture of Jesus's childhood which was not as important to the major themes of Matthew's gospel, but they do give us more insight into the humanity of Jesus which was a main emphasis of Luke's gospel.

Precursor

In writing this book, I have used scripture and, to a lesser extent, extrabiblical sources to speculate on how those who followed Jesus and those who opposed Him might have been affected by what they heard Him say and saw Him do. However, there is insufficient information to speculate about what those who lived in the home with Jesus as He grew up might have experienced. We know that Jesus had siblings, and we know that His mother Mary died sometime after He was crucified. We also know that Joseph was not mentioned in any of the narratives of Jesus as He came into His ministry or when He went to the cross, but Mary was mentioned in both. Most scholars believe that Joseph died several years prior to the crucifixion. We also know that James and Jude, two of the brothers of Jesus, contributed to the New Testament writing, but the only insight we have into life in the household of Joseph and Mary is found in Luke 2:39-52 when the family was on its annual road trip to Jerusalem.

Each year, the family traveled to the temple in Jerusalem for the Passover. During one of these annual family road trips from Nazareth to Jerusalem, Jesus turned up missing, and this sent Joseph and Mary into a panic. There is a lot to say about these 13 verses, and we will not delve into all of it, but as we attempt to better understand the impact Jesus had on those around Him, we absolutely must look at some of what God has provided through the lens of scripture here. Anyone who has taken a family road trip either as a parent or as a child can relate to this story.

By this point in Jesus's childhood, He certainly had younger siblings, and they would have consumed a considerable amount of Mary's time and attention during a long journey. The family made this annual journey with extended family, traveling in sort of a caravan. Jesus was twelve years old and nearly a man at this point. Mary was preoccupied with caring for the younger, more dependent children in the family. At some point Mary and Joseph realized it had been a while since anyone had seen Jesus. They looked among all the relatives, but no one had seen Him.

I can recall times during my childhood wherein I just blended in among my cousins during large family gatherings, so the situation is familiar. It had been at least 10 years since the last recorded instance wherein the messianic nature of Jesus had been confirmed in the temple or spoken of in a public setting. It is possible that by this point Joseph and Mary had settled into the routine of family life to the point where they did not give much thought to who Jesus was, but clearly, they were terrified that something had gone wrong when no one could find Him. (Luke 2:48) After three days, Mary and Joseph found Jesus in the temple.

Since becoming a Christian, I have heard it said over and over that ministry begins in the home, and such was certainly the case with Jesus. Again, there is very little we know about

Jesus as He grew into adulthood, but I imagine he would have been regarded as a young person who had very little interest in the things most young people were interested in. Rather than being amused by the things that captivated the attention of other boys His age, Jesus naturally gravitated toward things other kids probably had to be coaxed into investigating. Whereas the other kids looked forward to getting home and were excited to join the family caravan back to Nazareth, Jesus was fascinated by the temple. He was enamored by the teachers in the temple, and He was drawn to the things of God.

When Joseph and Mary found the boy Jesus, He was having adult conversations with the teachers in the temple. This is where Jesus felt at home, this is where He felt called to be, in the house of God, conversing with scholars about the things of God. When they saw Him, Mary was astonished, and although the scripture indicates that Jesus was having some deep conversations with the teachers, Mary was still a mother and her reaction to what she saw was typically motherly.

Upon seeing Jesus in the temple, Mary's question was, how could you do this to us, meaning, how could you remain behind without letting us know and causing us to worry? Jesus turned the inquisition around with a question of His own. My paraphrase of what Jesus asked His mother would be something like this. Why didn't you, of all people, know who I am and therefore, where I would be? It's almost as if Jesus was asking Mary why it took them three days to find Him when they should have known exactly where he would be if they understood who He was. As such, Jesus began His ministry by first presenting, in fact, revealing Himself to His family. (Luke 2:46-49) This was the last time scripture speaks of Jesus prior to Him becoming an adult. The next time we see Jesus, He was a grown man about to be baptized by John.

John The Baptizer

Jesus and John were separated in age by six months, and there is no indication that the two ever met prior to the day John baptized Jesus, other than their brief encounter when they were both still unborn. (Luke 1:41) The two finally met as John preached the gospel and baptized people in the Jordon River, warning his followers to repent and live lives of righteousness.

I would like to highlight here one of the many truly remarkable things about the Bible. God wanted a clear, definitive record of the beginning and end of Jesus's earthly ministry. Therefore, God gave us irrefutable historical data that can and has been corroborated by extra-biblical sources about when John preached in the wilderness and when he baptized Jesus. Look at the specificity offered in Luke 3:1-2. "***Now in the fifteenth year of the reign of Tiberius Caesar, when Pontius Pilate was governor of Judea, and Herod was tetrarch of Galilee, and his brother Phillip was tetrarch of the region of Iturea, and Trachonitis, and Lysanias was tetrarch of Abilene, in the high priesthood of Annas and Caiaphas, the word of God came to John, the son of Zacharias, in the wilderness***." This is like historians 2,000 years in the future saying, "***on the 11th day of the 9th month, in the 1st year of George W Bush, son of George H.W. Bush, when Guliani was governor of New York, John Paul II was Pope, and Bin-Laden was head of Al-Qaeda, the attacks in New York City, of the State of New York, in the United States of America, occurred***." With that much specificity, any historian could corroborate through multiple sources the date and the validity of the terrorist attack on the World Trade Center on September 11, 2001.

We know nothing about the childhood or early adulthood of John, but we do know that during the above-mentioned period, the word of God came to him, and he preached the gospel in the wilderness as he baptized those who came to him. While John baptized people in the Jordon River, he was approached by his relative, Jesus, and although John did not mention that they were related by blood, he did mention that Jesus was the promised Messiah. John was stunned by the presence of Jesus, and he immediately realized he was in the presence of greatness.

As we consider the impact Jesus had on those around Him, I think it is interesting that John and other relatives of Jesus never tried to exploit their family ties to Jesus for the purpose of bolstering their own standing among people. There is no record of Mary ever proudly referring to Jesus as her son, the Messiah. In all the accolades John bestowed upon Jesus, he never referred to Jesus as his relative. Even James and Jude, the brothers of Jesus, did not identify themselves as His brothers. Instead, we read James referring to himself as, "***A bondservant of God and of the Lord Jesus Christ***." (James 1:1) Jude, the other brother of Jesus referred to himself as, "***A bondservant of Jesus Christ, and brother of James***." (Jude 1:1) There is an implicit sense of reverent deference from John, James, and Jude as they build Jesus up and play down their own significance in His story.

Jesus went to the Jordon to be baptized, and while He was praying, heaven opened up, and the Holy Spirit came down and descended upon Him bodily like a dove, and a voice came out of heaven speaking to Jesus saying, "***You are My beloved Son, in You I am well-pleased***." (Luke 3:21-22).

When I visited Israel, my oldest son took me to the Jordon River, and there were church groups and individuals being baptized. It was a beautiful day, and I recall looking up just as a white dove swooped down on the river and then flew up and away. No doubt doves make this maneuver often, but for me it was an extraordinary experience. When the disciples of Jesus and John witnessed the Holy Spirit in bodily form as a dove descending on Jesus and the voice of God proclaiming Him as the Son of God, it was a life-changing experience for them. (Matthew 3:13-17)

The Messianic Agenda

Jesus was baptized in the district of Judea, in the Jordon River, near Bethany. (John 1:28) (Luke 3:3, 3:21-22) (Matthew 3:13-17) (Mark 1:9) After being baptized, Jesus began His public ministry in the vicinity where He was baptized. It was there that Jesus called His first disciples, including Andrew, Simon, Philip, and Nathanael. Jerusalem, where the temple was located, was also in the district of Judea, which included Bethlehem, Bethany, Emmaus, Arimathea, Ephraim, Jericho, and Hebron. After the baptism, Jesus decided to return from Judea and travel to the district of Galilee, where He grew up. (John 1:43) The district of Galilee included the cities of Nazareth, where Jesus lived during His childhood, Cana, where Jesus performed His first miracle, Tiberias, Magdala, Capernaum, and Chorazin.

Although Jesus's ministry did not begin in His hometown of Nazareth, His preaching and the miracles He performed in the other towns of Galilee caused considerable curiosity about who He was. As His fame grew through the things He taught, the healings He performed, and His confrontations with the religious authorities, Jesus and His disciples made their way north to Nazareth, the town where Jesus grew up. (Mark 1-6)

In much the same way that the gospel was brought to the Jews first, and then the rest of the world (Romans 1:16), Jesus revealed Himself first to the community where He grew up, and when they rejected Him, He continued on to those outside that community. This is why it is helpful to have some understanding of ancient Near Eastern geography. Think of the districts of Israel like counties within an American state, with each county being made up of several cities and townships. It is also helpful to understand that the word synagogue means gathering place, and the towns or communities within the district had their own synagogues. The temple in Jerusalem was a large place where all Jews gathered for sacrifice and worship, as they were able to do so, but the synagogues were local places of worship, often within the homes of prominent Jews.

Scripture tells us that after the baptism and temptation of Jesus, He returned to Galilee and news of Him spread throughout the district as He began teaching in ***their*** synagogues. Don't miss the fact that initially Jesus taught in the district of Galilee, but when scripture tells us He was teaching in their synagogues, it is an indication that while He was in the district of Galilee, He was not yet in His hometown of Nazareth, teaching in ***His*** synagogue. (Luke 4:14) However, when He came to the city of Nazareth, where He grew up, familiarity set in among the people He grew up with, and they rejected Him. Although Jesus initially taught in the synagogues of the communities surrounding Nazareth, He waited until He arrived in Nazareth to reveal His messianic identity and to share His messianic agenda.

Jesus not only taught in the synagogues of Galilee, but the first six chapters of Mark's gospel record several miracles Jesus performed there. It was at a wedding in Cana that Jesus turned water into wine, and although He began teaching, preaching, and performing miracles in the district of Galilee, near Nazareth, it was not until He arrived in Nazareth that He revealed His identity and His agenda.

In those days, the literate among the people would pass the scrolls of scripture around and read to everyone gathered. After being well received by the people in Galilee outside of Nazareth, when He came to His hometown of Nazareth, Jesus made the observation, "***A prophet is not without honor except in his hometown and among his own relatives and in his own household.***" (Mark 6:4)

In the Nazareth synagogue when they passed the scrolls to Jesus he turned to a passage in Issaiah 61:1-2 and read, "***The Spirit of the Lord is upon Me, because He anointed Me to preach the gospel to the poor, He has sent Me to proclaim release to the captives, and recovery of sight to the blind, to set free those who are oppressed, to proclaim the favorable year of the Lord.***" When Jesus closed the book and sat down, He said, "***Today this scripture has been fulfilled in your hearing.***" By reading these two verses of scripture, Jesus accomplished two things: He declared Himself as the promised Messiah, and He laid out His agenda for the next three years.

Our goal in this book is to put ourselves into the sandals of those who spent time with Jesus, both those who followed Him and those who opposed Him. Jesus presented Himself as the Messiah, and it is difficult to imagine a starker contrast than the reaction of awe and anticipation from those in the synagogues outside of Nazareth who did not know Him, and the rejection and disbelief from those in Nazareth who did know Him.

Everything we read in the Bible prepares us for our own encounter with the Savior, and there is nothing more damaging than the subtle, insidious, gnostic familiarity, which results in dismissal and rejection of the One who gave His life for us so that we can live. If we become so puffed up by our own toxic righteousness that we will not believe anything or anyone who does not fit our idea of Christ, we will not only miss out on our own salvation, but we will also miss the opportunity to lead others to Christ. This is the lesson of Jesus unveiling His messianic agenda; those who did not know Him embraced Him, and those who thought they knew Him rejected Him.

Sights Which Cannot Be Unseen

The phrase "Never a dull moment" certainly applies to the years the disciples spent with Jesus during His time on earth, but three of them witnessed one of the most awe-inspiring events in human history. By the first century, Moses and Elijah were larger-than-life characters in Jewish lore, and all the disciples of Jesus were aware of the role these men played in Jewish history. Given these facts, there is no way to fully comprehend what it meant for Peter, James, and John to see Jesus in an intense conversation with Moses and Elijah. Because we live in an age where technology restrains our capacity for being awestruck by grandiose images, it is easy to dismiss the impact this moment had on three simple, first-century fishermen who saw the unmistakable image of Moses and Elijah in their midst, speaking with Jesus about His impending departure. For the three disciples, this sight was breathtaking. (Matthew 17:1-8) (Mark 9:2-8)

By this point in His ministry, Jesus had already declared Himself to be the Messiah, and He had already performed multiple miracles, but none of this could compare to Him standing on a mountain top engaged in conversation with two of the best-known characters in Jewish history. This moment is significant in our quest to put ourselves in the inner circle of Jesus and to walk with the Messiah because of the ways in which this moment confirmed His messianic claim. When Jesus emerged from the baptismal waters, God the Father declared that He is the Messiah. Gathered among the people He grew up with, Jesus declared Himself as the Messiah. During the transfiguration, while Peter, James, and John observed, Moses and Elijah affirmed Jesus as the Messiah.

In chapter three, I described this moment in the life of Peter as one where he ought to have kept quiet. It is not my intention to be irreverent or overly critical of Peter; in fact, I think if I were in his place, I would have nervously offered some unnecessary or possibly incomprehensible utterance. But this was an unprecedented situation, and no one could have been prepared with a perfect response to it. Peter may have stuck his foot in his mouth on occasion, but his heart was usually in the right place.

As we consider the effect walking with Jesus had on those around Him, this is a moment worth paying some attention to. In this circumstance, the effect of what these men saw left them without a clear idea of what to say or what to do. Peter's response at least had an element of worship and reverence for the men that materialized before him on the mountain. Although I think it's worth asking what I might have done in that circumstance, I seriously doubt I could have come up with a better response. The desire of Peter's heart in that moment was to honor his Lord and to glorify God, but Peter's heart was further revealed when Jesus asked His disciples what they believed about His identity. (Matthew 15:15-1) (Mark 8:27-29)

Circumnavigating The Rumor Mill

Jesus made His way from Galilee toward Jerusalem, and wherever He went, there was talk and speculation about what He had said, what He had done, and who He was. The rumors about Jesus were plentiful, and everyone had an opinion, but when He sat down with His disciples and asked, " Who do people say that I am, He was not trolling for gossip, nor was He checking to see how many favorable comments people were making about Him. Jesus was asking His disciples if they were listening to what God revealed about Him, or if they were informed and influenced by the rumor mill

This conversation between Jesus and His disciples is recorded in the gospels of Matthew, Mark, and Luke. In all three gospels, when Jesus asked His disciples, " Who do you think I am, Peter answered correctly, saying, "***You are the Christ.***" In all three gospels, Jesus warned the disciples not to tell anyone who He was. However, Matthew records Jesus's follow-up comment to Peter, "***Blessed are you Simon Barjonah, for flesh and blood, [Human Beings] did not reveal this to you, but My Father who is in heaven***". Jesus was lauding Peter because he did not rely on gossip and rumor to inform his opinion about the identity of Jesus, instead, Peter believed what God revealed about His Son.

There is an important application for us in this passage. With social media and casual conversations, there is no shortage of opinions about who Jesus is. Just about everyone has an idea of who Jesus is and what it means to be a Christian. The interesting thing about both the opinions that come from outside the Christian church, and those that come from within the church, is that they are often based upon rumor, speculation, and folklore. Very few people prayerfully read and study the Bible to form their opinions about the words, deeds, identity, and mission of Jesus. As followers of Christ, like Peter, we need to be crystal clear about who Jesus is. (Mt 16:13-23, Lk 9:18-21, Mark 8:27-31)

When Jesus warned His disciples not to tell anyone that He is the Christ, He was not trying to conceal His identity; He wanted to reveal it. He wanted people to be informed by what they saw and what they heard. Jesus knew that His ministry would include great events of healing, feeding thousands, messages of hope, joy, love, and freedom, and He wanted everyone to know the heartfelt joy of hearing the voice of God beckoning them to discover His identity, rather than settling for whatever the rumor mill had to say. This is why it is so important for us, as disciples of Jesus, to strongly encourage people to study the Bible for themselves and to pray that God will reveal Himself as they study His Word.

As disciples of Jesus, we must carefully and prayerfully scrutinize any Christian movement that curtails or discourages individuals from reading and studying the Bible while pushing the teaching of some charismatic leader or group of leaders. We must also beware of any ministry that directs us to narrowly focus on certain segments of scripture presented out of context in exclusion to other scriptures and their biblical context.

Any movement that separates the people of God from the Word of God is false religion and ought to be resisted. Any movement that distorts the Word of God is false religion and ought to be resisted. These are ancient problems that Jesus confronted over and over again throughout the New

Testament. The religious authorities wanted to increase their power by establishing themselves as the only ones with accurate knowledge of God's Word, and these people crucified Jesus because He threatened their authority. Fifteen hundred years later, the protestant reformation was fought to restore the authority of the Bible in the Christian religion. Now, it falls to us to keep God's Word at the center of our faith.

- Remember the repeated phrase of Jesus when He was tempted by Satan after His 40-day fast, twice He said, "***It is written***." (Luke 4:4,8) At the third temptation, Jesus said, referring to Deuteronomy 6:16, "***It is said***." (Luke4:12)
- In Matthew 5, during the sermon on the mount, when Jesus spoke about the law regarding murder, He quoted Exodus 20:21,27.
- Confronting the Jewish authorities in Matthew 9:13 regarding His decision to eat with tax collectors, Jesus quoted Hosea 6:6.
- In Mark 10:7-8, Jesus responded to the Pharisees as they attempted to trap Him with a question regarding divorce. Jesus quoted Genesis 2:24.
- In Mark 12:29-30, when the Scribes asked Jesus what the great commandment is, Jesus quoted Deuteronomy 6:4-5.
- In Matthew 15:1-2, the Pharisees and scribes challenged Jesus because He broke their traditions. In verses 7-9, Jesus responded by quoting Isaiah 29:13.
- In Matthew 19:3, when He responded to the Pharisees regarding the permanence of marriage, Jesus quoted Genesis 1:27 and Genesis 2:24.

My point is that if Jesus recognized the power and importance of basing our theology on scripture, we should do the same because even with the very best of intentions, whenever we place the doctrines of popular preachers and Bible teachers above the Word of God, we build cults of false religion. Our thoughts on the identity of Jesus must be built on nothing less than His Word working in us with the indwelling Holy Spirit. These two, ***the Word of God*** and ***the Spirit of God, work in concert to reveal the nature, the power, and the presence of God.***

Nothing in this section is intended to suggest that Christians should not have opinions about Jesus or that we should not discuss our opinions of Jesus. The disciples of Jesus had opinions about who He was, and they discussed those opinions amongst themselves and with others. However, our opinions need to be informed by and grounded in the truth that comes from the Word of God and the Spirit of God. This is why, when I write, I do my best to include scriptural references to support what I have written, and I strongly suggest that you read what is written in this book in light of what you see in the scriptures. If, after reading the Word of God, you feel the Spirit of God leading you to a different conclusion, always defer to what God has revealed in His Word over anything written in this or any other book.

Journey's end

As we have moved through each chapter of this book, we continue to ask: How were those around Jesus affected by their walk with Him? In this section, I want to draw our attention to the reactions of the crowd and Jesus's inner circle when His journey from Galilee to Jerusalem came to an end. As Jesus made His triumphal entry into Jerusalem at the apex of His ministry, we see what may be the most jarring examples of Jesus's effect on those around Him. As usual, we may discover similarities between our own attitudes about Jesus and the reactions of those around the Messiah at this crucial point in time. I would like to specifically look at the reaction of Peter and the reaction of the crowds.

We must keep in mind that the gospel is not a sequence of events or stories to be told and then set aside. Like the journey undertaken by Jesus and His disciples from Galilee to Jerusalem, the gospel is truth, change, revelation, and restoration, in motion. Approaching Jerusalem meant nearing their final destination with Jesus both physically and metaphorically. Jesus brought His disciples from the place where His life as a human being began to the place where He laid down that life for all of us. Sharing the gospel with others is our opportunity to join Jesus in taking people from where they are toward their destiny in Christ. The final phase of this epic journey came with joyful shouts of adoration as people heralded the arrival of the chosen Messiah. (Matthew 21:1-11) (Mark 11:1-11) (Luke 19:28-44) The final phase also came with betrayal and abandonment when Jesus faced condemnation.

The adoration on display when Jesus made His triumphal entry into Jerusalem must be viewed in light of the frightening abandonment that followed. If we wish to see the portrait of Jesus as Messiah, we must open our eyes to both extremes. The crowds threw down their garments on the road as a donkey carrying Jesus made its way along the path. They shouted Hosanna, an expression of adoration, as He passed by. (Matthew 21:9) In their minds, they were witnessing their King, the chosen Messiah who would lead God's people. However, as Jesus was arrested, beaten, and accused, those same people abandoned Him and shouted "***crucify Him***" when Pilate offered them a choice. (Matthew 27:22)

Many things occurred between the triumphal entry of Jesus into Jerusalem and the trial which led to His crucifixion, but we can learn a great deal by observing the crowd as they watched their Messiah on top, riding into Jerusalem on a donkey, and how the same people regarded the same Messiah when trouble found Him. This is an uncomfortable truth about the human and even the Christian capacity for infidelity when our peace and security are threatened. Throughout the history of the Judeo-Christian faith, we have demonstrated great joy when celebrating a hero of the faith in triumph; when we are called to stand side-by-side with those same heroes during times of persecution, our tendency is to cower, hide, and even capitulate.

Jesus asked the question, "***Who do you say that I am***?" Peter nailed it because his knowledge of Jesus was conferred upon him by none other than God the Father. Jesus not only lauded Peter for this but also gave him a glimpse into his future ministry. Jesus knew that initially Peter would deny Him, but this knowledge did not change or in any way diminish the future ministry of Peter. Jesus told Peter that "***before the rooster crows, you will deny Me three times***". (Matthew 26:34) When Peter stood warming his hands in the courtyard, he heard the rooster crow after his third denial. In that moment, Peter felt conviction, but not condemnation. (Matthew 26:75)

Despite the fact that Jesus knew all His disciples would abandon Him (Matthew 26:56), He understood it was all part of the plan of redemption. Peter's denial of Jesus and the conviction he felt about that denial laid the foundation for his future faith and restoration. The crowds shouted,

"Crucify Him", yet when Jesus rose again, many of those who shouted, crucify Him, became committed followers of Christ. The conviction they experienced from denying Christ led to the revelation of Christ's grace, resulting in restoration through Christ. Jesus continues to make followers of those who deny Him today through the same process: conviction, followed by revelation and restoration.

It is amazing that Jesus was convicted by the courts of man without ever sinning, but He was never condemned by His Father. We, on the other hand, are convicted in our sin without condemnation from our Messiah. (Romans 8:1)

The Trial

Trials have always been about answering three essential questions:

1. Violation
    - Has the law been broken?
2. Conviction
    - Is there sufficient evidence to prove that the accused has broken the law?
3. Condemnation
    - What is the appropriate punishment for breaking the law?

This was the task before Caiphas, the high priest, then Herod, and finally Pilate. Ostensibly, their job was to determine if a law under their jurisdiction had been violated, examine the accused to determine if He was guilty, and assign an appropriate punishment. (Luke 23:1-25)

Caiaphas, who was the chief prosecutor for the Sanhedrin during the trail had already determined that Jesus needed to be found guilty of violating the Jewish law. For Caiaphas, the trial was simply a means of terminating Jesus's influence over the Jewish people. To this end, they tried to gather people who would testify against Jesus, but their stories were inconsistent. (Mark 14:55-59)

There is an irony in the strategy used by the Sanhedrin. As interpreters and guardians of the law, they put Jesus on trial for blasphemy which is a derivative of the 3rd commandment, "***You shall not take the name of the Lord your God in vain***." (Exodus 20:7) Their position was that by claiming to be the Son of God, (Messiah), Jesus was taking the Lord's name in vain. The inconvenient truth is that Jesus's claim to be the Son of God is true, but the tactic they deployed to trap Jesus was a violation of the 9th commandment, "***You shall not bear false witness against your neighbor***." (Exodus 20:16) The 9th commandment is often misrepresented as a commandment not to lie, but it specifically prohibits giving false testimony in a criminal trial because in so doing an innocent person can be convicted and then sentenced to death, which is exactly what happened to Jesus. The irony is that while claiming to defend the law, the religious authorities violated the law in a most egregious way.

Once Jesus boldly claimed to be the Son of God, Caiaphas was satisfied that all three essential questions had been answered. In his judgment, the Mosaic law had been violated, Jesus was the guilty party, and the appropriate punishment was death. However, as a Jew living in the occupied territories of Rome, Caiaphas had no authority to hand down a death sentence. For a death sentence, Caiaphas would need to convince the Roman government that punishing Jesus for violating this Mosaic law was in the best interest of Rome. Therefore, Caiaphas needed to make the case that by breaking the Jewish laws, Jesus had committed the crime of sedition and that it was in the best interest of the Roman Government to hand down a death sentence.

Jesus was then sent to Pilate, who wanted nothing to do with the matter. As soon as Pilate learned that Jesus was from Galilee and that Herod, who had jurisdiction over that district, was in Jerusalem, he sent Jesus to Herod. Herod had no interest in ruling on this matter; his primary interest was in seeing if Jesus would perform one of His famous miracles for his amusement. (Luke 23:8-12)

As always, I encourage you to read the biblical narrative for yourselves, and when you do, try not to miss the way Jesus dealt with each of the three courts that put Him on trial. Caiaphas, the one who desperately wanted a conviction and death sentence, used every dirty trick he could come up with, and yet he could not trump up the charges against Jesus. Only when Jesus spoke for Himself was there sufficient evidence to convict Him on the bogus charge of blasphemy. Herod, who was only interested in his own amusement, got nothing out of Jesus and found no grounds to punish Him. Pilate had to get Jesus to self-incriminate by asking Him if He was king of the Jews, to which Jesus replied, "***It is as you say***." (Luke 23:3) With this admission, Jesus had affirmed what the Sanhedrin accused Him of, but even Pilate understood that the confession did not warrant a death sentence.

My point is that the trial was never a matter of convicting Jesus for His own crimes; it was always about Jesus being convicted for our sins. Further, the life of Jesus was never taken from Him; He walked willingly and purposely into the conviction and punishment for our sakes, not for the sake of His accusers but for the sake of those who seek a Messiah. (John 10:17-18)

Nothing Jesus said was sufficient to warrant a death sentence, so in order to appease the crowd, Pilate came up with an alternate solution. First, Pilate had Jesus beaten severely, and when that did not satisfy the bloodlust of His accusers, Pilate offered the crowd a choice: either Jesus or the notorious criminal Barabbas could be set free; the crowd chose Barabbas. (Luke 23:13-25)

If nothing else, the trial of Jesus makes it clear that His conviction was spurious, and while the punishment fit our crimes, Jesus was without guilt. The trial and subsequent conviction of Jesus were the culmination of His messianic role. By offering Himself to be convicted and crucified as the perfect human, Jesus fulfilled His role as deliverer. This is the incredible covenant we have with our Lord; we are guilty, but He takes the punishment for that guilt. "***Therefore, there is now no condemnation for those who are in Christ Jesus***." (Romans 8:1) The effect of Jesus willingly presenting Himself as the sacrificial lamb continues to this day, but it began after the crucifixion as His disciples transitioned into apostles.

Turning Disciples Into Apostles

The word disciple means learner, and the word apostle means sent. Jesus spent 3 years developing learners, and then He sent them to make learners of the rest of the world. Most Christians are aware of the Great Commission in Matthew 28:19. After three years of teaching, coaching, correcting, guiding, and loving His disciples, Jesus laid down His life. On the third day, He rose from the dead, proving conclusively that He is the Messiah, God incarnate, and that the grave could not hold Him. After laying down His life, rising from the dead, and being seen by hundreds, Jesus gave the disciples the great commission, which turned them from disciples into apostles.

As a new Christian, I assumed that Matthew 28:19 was a call to make converts, but it is so much more than that. The disciples returned to Galilee, where their journey with Jesus started. Jesus gathered the 11 disciples and said, "***All authority has been given to Me in heaven and on earth***." (Matthew 28:18) This was said to set up the mission He was about to send them on. Jesus then spoke the great commission, "***Go therefore, [Because all authority has been given to Me] and make disciples of all the nations, baptizing them in the name of the Father and the Son and the Holy Spirit, teaching them to observe all that I commanded you; and lo, I am with you always, even to the end of the age.***"

The basis for the Great Commission was that Jesus had been granted all authority by the Father. With that authority, Jesus converted the learners into teachers, sending them out to teach everything they had learned from the master. Notice, Jesus did not say go and convert pagans into Christians; such a limited view of the great commission is what makes many missionary and evangelism efforts ineffective. The goal was never to convert; it was always to make students.

A limited, "conversion only" understanding of the great commission creates a passive and ineffective Christian because once a person is saved, there is little more for the converted person to do. However, when a disciple is made, conversion is perpetual, and it involves constant study and interaction with both believers and non-believers. This is another reason it is so vital for the Christian to continue to study the Bible, because this is what identifies us as disciples or students, our continued pursuit of the knowledge and wisdom of God, coupled with the ongoing process of conversion.

Jesus commanded the newly commissioned disciples to make disciples of all nations. The word nations is a translation of the Greek word ethne, which means ethnicity or people group. In other words, Jesus was not speaking of national borders; He was speaking of people as defined by their ethnicity, culture, and geography. Jesus was commanding His disciples, and this includes all of us, to share and teach the gospel to all ethnicities within our local communities and around the world. Of all the things the disciples had heard from Jesus, this would have been one of the most challenging because they had always believed that the gospel was exclusively for the Jews. However, it was not until a few years after the ascension of Christ that Paul, in collaboration with Peter, challenged the church to get on board with the expansive nature of the great commission. (Acts 10, 11, 15:1-12)

The Book of Acts marks the beginning of the church age, and although the book is complete, the acts of the apostles are ongoing, continuing to this day with you and with me. The Acts of the Apostles is a book of the Bible that gives us an amazing look at the church's beginnings and how the gospel spread by the power of the Holy Spirit. Jesus appears corporally in Acts 1 as He handed the mantle of ministry to the apostles, and He appeared posthumously, speaking to Saul as he walked the road to Damascus. (Acts 9:3-16)

As we arrive at the conclusion of this book, I must concede that the effect Jesus had on the lives of those within His inner circle and those on the periphery eludes my best attempts to describe. The Bible provides us with an account of what they did, and we can do our best to imagine how they felt in His presence, but I think in the end we realize the most amazing attribute of Jesus is that whether we lived in the 1st century and saw Him physically, or we live in the 21st century and see Him through the pages of the Bible, we are moved to repentance and aspire to bring Him glory.

Epilogue

The Apostle Peter is a compelling figure to study. Of all the Apostles, with the notable exception of Paul, the personality and character of Peter are more fully developed in the Bible than any of the others. I think most of us can, to some degree, identify with Peter, and many of us would love to have the impact on Christianity that Peter had. This uneducated fisherman with a relentless desire to impress and please our Lord Jesus is a man with an endearing personality, to say the least.

If you are anything like me, you have noticed the dramatic difference between the Peter who stood outside the High Preist's house, warming his hands by the fire, cursing, and denying that he even knew Jesus, to the man of the hour on the Day of Pentecost a short time later, preaching the fiery sermon with clarity and conviction before the masses. The question in all our minds is, "How did Peter transform in such a brief period of time?"

It has been argued, even by me, that it was the indwelling of the Holy Spirit that accounts for the man we see on Pentecost and throughout the balance of the New Testament, but I would like to propose an alternative theory. This is not to argue against the power of the Holy Spirit in the life of Peter and in the lives of all the apostles, but I offer not so much a counterargument as a supplemental one. I propose that it was the Holy Spirit working in concert with the risen Jesus that transformed Peter from the bumbling, vacillating, impetuous, pre-Pentecost disciple to the Apostle Peter, the rock on which Jesus built His church.

In chapter six, we discussed John 21, where Peter and the other disciples encountered the risen Christ by the seashore and how Jesus used Peter's brokenness to develop him from a disciple into an apostle. As Peter jumped from the boat and ran onto the shore into Jesus's waiting arms, He experienced the culmination of everything Jesus had been teaching him for those three years; he experienced Jesus, who once was dead and buried, having risen from the grave, just as He said He would. Over a three-year period, Jesus went from being a theological, doctrinal construct of all that could be in the mind of Peter, to the fulfillment of everything promised and everything He ever would be. Peter's journey led him to a profound personal encounter with God incarnate in the person of Jesus Christ.

Throughout my Christian life, I have heard people speak about their love for Jesus, and I have even heard people talk and sing about being in love with Jesus. As I set out to write this book, I wanted to know that kind of excited and enthusiastic love for my Lord and Savior because I felt I was missing something, and I didn't want to miss anything in my journey with Christ. I wanted to experience loving Jesus the way I saw others loving Him in church and in worship services. To be honest, I did not feel the way others seemed to feel who were "On fire for Jesus". Somewhere along the way, while working on this book, I had a paradigm shift that allowed me to discover my own genuine love for the Lord.

The King James version of the Bible translates Jesus's words in John 14:15 as, "***If ye love Me, keep My commandments***." The NASB version translates the verse as, "***If you love Me, you will keep My commandments.***" Whereas the King James Version suggests that Jesus is saying, "If you love Me, I am directing you to keep My commandments," the NASB version implies that Jesus is saying, "If you love Me, evidence of that love will be seen in your desire to keep My commandments." This is similar to what we discovered in chapter 6 when we looked at John 15:10, where Jesus said, "***If you keep my commandments, you will abide in My love***." As we discussed in chapter 6, Jesus was not saying that keeping His commandments was a condition of loving Him; He was saying that keeping His commandments would enable one to love Him. For many, this is a distinction without a difference, yet for others, including myself, the distinction represents a monumental difference. I want to offer an anecdote that may help to make my point.

I met a young Muslim man recently whose parents were born in Somalia. The young man was deeply devout; he prayed 5 times a day, attended the mosque regularly, and observed Ramadan each year. Someday, this young man plans to marry a Muslim girl and raise his family according to the teachings of Islam. I asked him why someone so young was so devoted to his faith, and he told me that since he was a child, he had observed the conduct of his parents and other elders, and he had been the beneficiary of their love, providence, and protection. The young man explained that he wanted to make his family proud and to demonstrate his love for them through his devout behavior. This young man was not devout because he was commanded to show his love; he was devout as a demonstration of his love.

There is no question that Jesus issued commandments to His disciples, and because we are His disciples, these commandments are passed down to us. However, in John 14:15, Jesus is not commanding us to keep His commandments; He is saying that our love for Him will compel us to do so. During the dialogue between Jesus and

Peter by the seashore in John 21:15-17, Jesus, using the word agape, the highest expression of love, asks Peter three times if he is ready to profess this grandiose expression of love for Him. After each instance, Jesus simply tells Peter to obey Him; no grand gestures, grand speeches, no bold confessions of fealty, just obey. This dialogue between Jesus and Peter is propositional. Jesus is saying don't just tell me you love me, show me by your enthusiastic and sacrificial willingness to obey Me. Jesus doubled down on this proposition in verses 18-23, where He challenged Peter to follow Him as a demonstration of his love. Peter was to follow Jesus even in the manner in which he would die as a demonstration of his love.

In these passages, Jesus was simply drawing our attention to a basic tenet of human behavior that has drawn people to false religion since the beginning of time but can and should also be used to draw us toward Him. From the beginning of humanity, people have been drawn away from God by charismatic leaders, lofty ideas, and vain, empty philosophy, all of which led to death, but Jesus has come to bring life. Put another way, Jesus is saying, when you truly love Him, you will be drawn irresistibly to keep His commandments.

My paradigm shift was this: love for Jesus is not demonstrated in our style or form of worship, nor is it revealed in gushy, even energetic, gregarious enthusiasm. Love for Jesus is revealed in our persistent and dogged determination to follow His commandments, even when doing so costs us everything. Once I understood this truth, although I had known since the day of my salvation that Jesus loved me, I knew without a doubt that I love Jesus regardless of how I feel at any given moment and regardless of what others might infer from my style of worship.

I therefore challenge you to continue your study of the Bible and learn what it means for you to follow Jesus and to obey His commandments. I challenge you to follow Him even when the cost of following is higher than you ever imagined. Meditate on the words of Jesus in Matthew 10:34 and other passages where Jesus warns us that following Him is costly, but worth the cost. I challenge you to embrace the truth that the Bible is not written to bring you comfort but to help you develop courage. Because if you are a follower of Jesus, you will need courage. Your love for Jesus is revealed in your persistent devotion to Him despite the trouble your devotion brings.

I pray that our journey of discovering Jesus, seeing Him for who He really is, and knowing Him as He was known by those who walked with Him will begin a transformation in us. I pray that all the bluster, all the catchy Christian sound bites, all the biblically based platitudes, and even scripture memorization would no longer serve as a substitute for an encounter with the real Jesus. As you lay down this book and return to the familiar rhythm of life, I pray that you will see Jesus on the seashore, broiling the fish, baking the bread, and waiting for you with open arms of love. I pray that when He looks you in the eye and asks if you love Him, as Peter did, you will drop any pretense and answer Him honestly so that your own transformation may begin. By the power of the Holy Spirit, may the beauty of our risen Savior captivate you and set you free to share the love of Christ with the world.

Biography

Doug Belton

Doug Belton is a Christian writer with a deep and abiding passion for the Bible. Doug attended Dallas Theological Seminary for his graduate studies majoring in historical theology. Doug's graduate thesis entitled, "The Puritan Hope" traces the pilgrim migration of 1623 from England to the newly formed colonies of America. His first published book is a fast paced and exciting Christian crime novel available through Amazon Books under the name Eve Ann by D.W. Belton. Doug lives in the Twin Cities of Minnesota. He is the father of six adult children, eight grandchildren, and two great grandchildren.

www.ingramcontent.com/pod-product-compliance
Lightning Source LLC
LaVergne TN
LVHW050517100826
845148LV00002B/365

* 9 7 9 8 2 3 4 0 1 4 7 4 0 *